SCREEN EPIPHANIES

SCREEN EPIPHANIES

film-makers on the films that inspired them

Geoffrey Macnab

A BFI book published by Palgrave Macmillan

First published in 2009 by
PALGRAVE MACMILLAN

on behalf of the

BRITISH FILM INSTITUTE
21 Stephen Street, London W1T 1LN
www.bfi.org.uk

There's more to discover about film and television through the BFI. Our world-renowned archive, cinemas, festivals, films, publications and learning resources are here to inspire you.

Palgrave Macmillan in the UK is an imprint of Macmillan Publishers Limited, registered in England, company number 785998, of Houndmills, Basingstoke, Hampshire RG21 6XS. Palgrave Macmillan in the US is a division of St Martin's Press LLC, 175 Fifth Avenue, New York, NY 10010. Palgrave Macmillan is the global academic imprint of the above companies and has companies and representatives throughout the world. Palgrave® and Macmillan® are registered trademarks in the United States, the United Kingdom, Europe and other countries.

Cover design: couch
Cover image: (front) *Room at the Top* (Jack Clayton, 1958, Remus Films); (back) *The Blue Angel* (Josef von Sternberg, 1930, Ufa)
Stills courtesy of BFI Stills, Posters and Designs
Set by Cambrian Typesetters, Camberley, Surrey/couch
Printed in China

This book is printed on paper suitable for recycling and made from fully managed and sustained forest sources. Logging, pulping and manufacturing processes are expected to conform to the environmental regulations of the country of origin.

British Library Cataloguing-in-Publication Data
A catalogue record for this book is available from the British Library

ISBN 978-1-84457-190-1 (hbk)

Contents

Acknowledgments

I would like to thank my editor, Rebecca Barden, for her patience and encouragement. I would also like to thank all the staff at the BFI who have helped with this book in various ways: Brian Robinson, Geoff Andrew and the late Anthony Minghella (who put me in touch with some of the film-makers interviewed here). I am very grateful to Sophia Contento for her picture research and layout design, and to Suzanne Fowler for her enthusiastic publicity and marketing.

Introduction

A working-class kid (Alan Parker) playing on a north London street in the 1950s steals away to watch a scratchy, second-run film in a fleapit cinema on Essex Road, Islington. He is mesmerised by what he sees. This is a film made in New York about boy roughly his own age who takes the train to Coney Island to escape trouble at home. The little English kid, growing up in austerity-era Britain, can't believe the sheer abundance characterising the lives on screen – the cars, the skyscrapers, the colour, the vitality.

In the mid-1950s, a London teenager (David Puttnam), who will one day become Britain's best-known film producer, identifies very closely with Montgomery Clift and James Dean. The Oedipal tension, the teen rebellion, the hair, the lithe and dynamic performance style all register strongly with him. What he can't fathom, though, is how James Dean always seems to drive away in a car. Teenagers in 1950s Enfield didn't have cars.

At home alone one evening while his parents are out, a nine-year-old boy (Anthony Minghella) stumbles on an old black-and-white movie on TV. He is both aroused and horrified by its subject matter. It is a film about sexual and social humiliation. Marlene Dietrich tantalises a pompous teacher until he is reduced to the status of a clown. So this is the way adults behave, the boy thinks to himself. If he is appalled, he is also intensely curious, and can begin to understand the motivations of both the teacher and the femme fatale. Doesn't Dietrich look appealing up there on stage, with those long legs, those suspenders and that top hat? In his own, preadolescent way, the boy can sense the erotic lives of these grown-ups: the pleasure and the misery they give one another.

The anarchist's daughter (Sally Potter) isn't allowed to see many films but there is something about Jacques Tati and the Marx brothers that bowls her over every time – a zest, an orchestrated chaos and (to her mind) a melancholy too. The industrialist's son (Manoel De Oliveira), who would go on to become the world's oldest working film director, is similarly affected when he is taken to see Charlie Chaplin movies.

In 1980s Southall, a British girl of Indian origin (Gurinder Chadha) is trying to work out her own identity. Her relatives in India frown on the perceived decadence of western life: the women in miniskirts, the men in their flowery shirts. They fear that the Indians in Britain are being corrupted, that the 'younger generation' will forget all about the battle for independence and the discipline and sacrifice demonstrated by their parents. Besides, the UK is a country of overt racism. She sees her own father – a highly educated man – continually passed over for promotion. For all these reasons, a film by an Indian director about the British-Asian experience has an extraordinary resonance for her. While she may not agree with the film's attitudes toward its characters or its tendency toward caricature, here is a movie that both entertains her and speaks to her about the issues in her own life.

The above instances are all 'epiphanies' included in this book: key formative experiences in the lives of future film-makers. The term 'epiphany' might be – as the film-maker Ken Loach contends on these pages – a little on 'the heavy breathing side'. The idea that someone is so overwhelmed by an individual film that it changes their lives and turns them, almost instantly, into a movie director is, perhaps, far-fetched. For most of the interviewees here, it was not a case of a single 'Rosebud' moment.

The Rosebud parallel is instructive, though. In Orson Welles's *Citizen Kane*, the word whispered on the dying tycoon's lips promises, at first, to unveil the mystery of his life. Of course, it does no such thing.

It's a storytelling device – what Alfred Hitchcock might have called a McGuffin. It sets the plot in motion. Kane's wildly contradictory personality can't be explained away or summed up by a single word. Nevertheless, the word is a hint: Rosebud is the name on the childhood sledge that we see burned at the end of the movie. It's the door that leads to Kane's past. The same might be observed of many of the 'epiphanies' the film-makers discuss here. The richness of their observations lies not just in the film, or moment in a film, but in the way it helps to conjure up other details of their filmgoing pasts.

The British film-makers included here who grew up in the 1950s evoke a world that seems very distant to anyone watching movies today. The Nottingham described by Stephen Frears, the Manchester and London evoked by Mike Leigh, the north London suburbs of David Puttnam's early cinemagoing years or the Liverpool that Terence Davies waxes nostalgic about are all cities where cinemas seem to be on every street. There are first-run houses and second-run houses, old picture palaces and fleapits. The number of films available to watch is mind-boggling.

Many discuss the impact of being in at the birth of the New Wave. Whereas in the 1950s, the diet for British cinemagoers consisted primarily of Hollywood and British films, the 60s – at least in London – saw a sudden rush of films sharing the same rebellious sensibility from directors in France, Italy, Eastern Europe and even the UK. Jean-Luc Godard and Ingmar Bergman were cited by many as standard-bearers of a new approach to cinema. However, the devotion to these auteurs wasn't necessarily deep-rooted. Indeed, some interviewees express exasperation at the route Godard took, losing interest in his work when he entered his Maoist phase. Others eventually began to feel that Bergman and Michelangelo Antonioni were too earnest and self-important. Nonetheless, during the late 1950s and early 60s, these directors were inspirational figures for a younger generation.

The interviewees here often talk about their 'epiphanies' in terms of the getting of knowledge. In their childhoods, films were simply 'there', projected on the screen as if by magic. Most had little notion that these films were 'made'. Editing, cinematography, sound, lighting, make-up, music, special effects and every other part of the craft were unknown to the young cinemagoers. They saw movies as unmediated, magnified reality. Even when they did question the device, they would do so in a naive fashion. Animator Nick Park recalls being startled as a kid by the way that cars drove off cliffs in action movies. Those stunt drivers, he thought, must have been very brave, very foolhardy or very well paid to accept certain death for the sake of the movie. For some, the discovery of the craft and artifice behind the films is a source of disappointment and disillusionment. Just like Dorothy when she learns that the Wizard of Oz is just a wizened, tubby man behind a curtain, they feel short-changed. For others, the contrivance is itself magical. They begin to have the sense that they, too, could create something akin to this.

For many of the interviewees, growing up in provincial working-class England, the very notion of becoming a film-maker seemed impossibly far-fetched. With no film schools or apprenticeships, the British industry seemed to be the preserve of a privileged few working in the south-east. Hollywood, meanwhile, was a different galaxy altogether. Nonetheless, seeing a particular film at a particular time somehow set them on a road that would eventually lead them to emerge as directors themselves.

As children and young adults, the Britons interviewed here invariably seemed to have preferred American films to those produced in their own backyard, hating the plummy voices of the British movie stars and the irritating fake cockney accents of actors in working-class roles. Although Terence Davies argues persuasively that post-war British screen comedy (Ealing films, movies with Margaret Rutherford and Alastair Sim) was superior – and funnier – than its American equivalents, his passion as a kid was primarily for Technicolor Doris Day musicals. Lord Puttnam likewise opted first for Hollywood fare. British films were the second or third choice – something to be watched when that week's choice of American titles had been exhausted. What is striking among the older interviewees, though, is the sheer primacy of cinemagoing as a leisure activity. They had a huge appetite for films partly because there was so little else for them to do. At the same time, films weren't fetishised as they are today. They weren't available to be downloaded, watched on YouTube, paused, rewound and explored again and again. Many of the 'epiphanies' here relate to films – or moments in films – that the interviewees saw just once, which only adds to the intensity of the memory they are trying to conjure up. Indeed, they are often able to recall the precise circumstances in which they saw the movie, describing the flock wallpaper in the theatre, the route they took to get to the cinema or even the seats they sat in. One (Don Boyd) gives a surreal description of watching Laurence Olivier's *Hamlet* outdoors in the African desert at twilight. Others offer vivid and sometimes comic accounts of the flourishing repertory system of the 1950s. Stephen Frears claims to have been able to hear lions roaring from the circus next door while watching films at one cinema in Nottingham. Mike Leigh speaks with a mix of affection and disgust of the Tolmer Cinema near Warren Street tube station in London, a place where homeless people and prostitutes congregated. Steeped with the pervasive stench of alcohol and piss, it was also a place where you could sometimes see great foreign-language movies at bargain rates. Alan Parker recalls the semi-organised mayhem of Saturday-morning children's screenings.

Younger film-makers will often have had the opportunity to see films again and again. Lars von Trier confides that he has only seen Stanley Kubrick's *Eyes Wide Shut* twice and that he would really need to watch it again to make up his mind about it.

Most of the interviewees here are looking back into film history. Some of the younger ones – directors like Kevin Macdonald and Nick Park – turn to Powell and Pressburger and to Hitchcock. Indeed, the most recent films discussed here are already at least thirty years old: Francis Ford Coppola's *Apocalypse Now*, George Lucas's *THX 1138* and Terrence Malick's *Badlands*. The attraction of Coppola's Vietnam epic lies as much in the way it was made as the film itself. Coppola famously went into the jungle, risked madness, fought with his financiers and pushed himself to extremes to complete the movie. For both Thomas Vinterberg and Danny Boyle, it was precisely that crusading element – that monomania – that made the film so compelling.

I embarked on this book with the idea that leading film-makers would be able to remember a moment in their filmgoing career when everything suddenly made sense. The hope was that they would talk in detail about just how and when they had their cinematic 'epiphany'. Von Trier's own choice, Kubrick's *Barry Lyndon*, initially seems surprising. The maverick Dane behind Dogme 95, with its emphasis on handheld camerawork, natural lighting and a freewheeling approach, plumps for Kubrick's most studied and stately film – a literary adaptation in which the period details are foregrounded in an obsessive way.

The interviewees here have often discussed more than a single film. Asked about their 'epiphany', they have responded by talking in intimate detail about their childhood cinemagoing or about how they took their first teetering steps in the film industry. They have spelled out the hurdles they had to overcome because of race or class or gender. For some, the moment of epiphany was not a specific film but the people they met or experiences they had at formative moments in their film-making careers. The interviewees come from very different backgrounds. They range from the great Portuguese auteur Manoel De Oliveira (who had turned one hundred two months before I spoke to him) to the Oscar-winning Danny Boyle.

Certain directors I approached were resistant to being interviewed on the grounds that it was too reductive to narrow their many key formative experiences in cinema to a single 'epiphany'. 'I really don't think in terms of scenes. Films have a cumulative effect on me. I am reminded of what the cameraman on my first feature said: "You have to be careful as a cameraman, one good shot can ruin a bad film,"' the director John Boorman responded as he declined to take part. Others fretted about the religious connotation of 'epiphany' and worried about seeming too self-important or portentous.

Thankfully, many film-makers were more forthcoming and were often prepared to set aside many hours from their busy lives to share their cinematic 'epiphanies'. I would like to express my gratitude to them. It is their book more than it is mine.

Directors / Epiphanies

Kevin Macdonald

The Life and Death of Colonel Blimp

(Michael Powell and
Emeric Pressburger, 1943)

Kevin Macdonald
filming *The Last
King of Scotland*
(2007)

Kevin Macdonald comes from a family steeped in cinema history. His older brother Andrew is the producer of *Trainspotting* (1996) and *Shallow Grave* (1994). His uncle, James Lee, was briefly the Chief Executive of Goldcrest. His grandfather was Emeric Pressburger, the Hungarian-born screenwriter who came to Britain in the mid-1930s and went on to work with director Michael Powell on a series of films, many of which are now acknowledged as classics of British cinema. These range from *The Life and Death of Colonel Blimp* (1943) to *The Red Shoes* (1948).

Macdonald, who grew up in Scotland, began his professional career as a writer and book editor, working for Faber. He co-edited *Imagining Reality: The Faber Book of Documentary*. In the early 1990s, he wrote a biography of Pressburger, *The Life and Death of a Screenwriter*. This spawned a TV documentary about his grandfather that he presented and directed. Slowly, Macdonald moved into film-making, working on documentaries about Howard Hawks and Donald Cammell. His breakthrough came with the Oscar-winning *One Day in September* (1999), a feature documentary exploring the background to the slaying of the Israeli athletes at the 1972 Munich Olympics by the Palestinian group Black September. In that film, as in its successor, *Touching the Void* (2003), a documentary based on Joe Simpson's book about his ill-fated mountain expedition in the Peruvian Andes in the mid-1980s, Macdonald unapologetically used devices and ideas more commonly found in dramatic features than in conventional documentaries. His work was aimed at the big screen. Rock music, reconstructions and stylised editing were all thrown into the mix as he tried to ensure his films had impact.

Having successfully made feature documentaries, Macdonald took the leap into fiction when he directed *The Last King of Scotland* (2006). A drama based on real events that occurred in Uganda in the 1970s under the dictatorship of Idi Amin, the film won an Oscar for its star Forest Whitaker, who played Amin. His next film was *State of Play* (2009), a thriller set against the backcloth of the journalistic world. Ironically, Macdonald himself had once thought about becoming a journalist, before dismissing the idea because the profession was so poorly paid.

Perhaps unsurprisingly, the personable Macdonald cited one of his grandfather's best-known films, *Colonel Blimp*, as his epiphany. A Jewish Eastern European who had become part of the great émigré tide heading westward during the Hitler years, Pressburger might easily have ended up in Hollywood like his contemporaries from the Berlin years, Billy Wilder and Fred Zinnemann. Instead, he stayed in Britain and became more British than the Brits themselves. *Colonel Blimp* is one of the great films about Englishness, both in its idealised form (as a young man, the film's hero Clive Wynne-Candy epitomises notions of decency and gallantry) and also at its most reactionary. The irony was not only that it was written by a Hungarian but that Pressburger himself, in the latter part of his life, would end up just as neglected and marginalised as the walrus-moustached Blimp.

Kevin Macdonald:

" I grew up in the countryside in Scotland, a million miles from anything cinematic. My grandfather was this very distant figure in my life. I was told, as I was growing up, that he had made films. They weren't films that really appealed to a child. They weren't Walt Disney. Nor were they action movies or Westerns or *Lawrence of Arabia*. I wasn't particularly interested in them. I remember there was a season of his films in about 1977. We rented a VCR machine, which was a very hi-tech piece of equipment at that time, and recorded all the films. I tried to watch them, but except for *The Spy in Black* and *Contraband*, which had a certain derring-do, I found them dull. I never really spoke to my grandfather about the films. I never really thought about going into films myself.

Then, I went to university at Oxford. I was eighteen or nineteen. A year or two later, my grandfather had become very ill and had gone into an old people's home. My brother and I were in the strange position of being his only relatives. My mother wasn't really in contact with him. We felt responsible for this old man, who was in his eighties. I had a strong emotional bond with him even though I hadn't spent a lot of time with him in childhood. I went to see him every few months in his old people's home. For a young person to see him in that setting, it was quite upsetting. There was something a bit pathetic about his situation. He was somebody who had led an extraordinary life and who had ended up alone with no relatives apart from his two grandchildren. The old people's home was in Diss in Suffolk, of all places.

There was a film club at Oxford. One Saturday afternoon, they showed *The Life and Death of Colonel Blimp*. I said to friends we've got nothing else to do, let's go and see that. I think because he was unwell and shortly after that died, I was particularly emotionally open to the film. I sat there and it was a sort of epiphany. I realised that this wasn't just a very good film but that he [my grandfather] was a film-maker of genius and this was one of the best films I had ever seen. Not only that, but I could see – because I was very attuned to him and his story – so much of him in the film. I realised that this film had come out of his own own life and his experiences. It wasn't just that one of the characters was a refugee and an émigré from Germany, as he was. It wasn't just because the film had his attitudes toward Churchill and Britain in it. There was also

something deeper than that. It had his emotion in it – something of him that was very personal. It is about a man who, at different times, falls in love rather hopelessly with three girls. They are all played by Deborah Kerr. It was a very bold decision to do that. As a child, I remember thinking, what is the point in that? But it suddenly came to me when I was watching the film and saw Deborah Kerr appear again and again that there was some deep truth to that about him and his life: a romantic pessimism that he had – a sense that romance never quite comes off. You are always looking for an ideal. The third time, when this ideal woman played by Deborah Kerr appears, she is an ambulance driver in the war. Her name is Angela. When she appears, the character Theo [Anton Walbrook] says: 'What a lovely name. It comes from angel, doesn't it?' I knew my mother's name is Angela. Suddenly, it all made sense to me on a personal level. I looked up when the film was made and it turned out that he wrote that script in the month his daughter was born.

In his diary, my grandfather writes about his wooing of Mrs Green. She was my grandmother. He had an unsuccessful relationship with her and was divorced after ten years or less than

that. He had a daughter he never saw again – my mother. It was all taking place in the war years. I think the interesting thing about Powell and Pressburger's films, as well as those of Launder and Gilliat and Humphrey Jennings, is that they made their best work in the war. People really were motivated by something other than their own careers. There was a desire to say something important, to do something important that would last. Film can be of great importance. It can change the attitude of people. It can entertain them in a difficult world. People [in the war] lived their lives to the full and at full tilt. People had affairs all over the place. It was a sexually liberated period. That didn't happen again until the 60s. People think that the 60s were so sexually open, but it was much more so during the war – there was this sense that this might be your last opportunity. That heightened people not just sexually but artistically too. People felt there was a reason to really push themselves. Powell and Pressburger made their best films in the war or in the immediate shadow of the war, in reaction to what they had been through.

Blimp is also a film about how the young can't understand the old and

The Life and Death of Colonel Blimp

how young people think they know best. They think the old people are so out of touch and outmoded. There is that lack of communication between people who've lived a long life and those who are starting out in life. The film operates on a cerebral level as well as an emotional level. It's funny, it's visually flamboyant, it has got everything in it. For me, it is my lodestone as a great movie. I am loath to say it is my favourite movie but for me it has the most significance of any film.

I realised that the construction of *Colonel Blimp*, which I had thought was rather odd, was brilliant and extraordinarily bold. It had seemed random to me before, but there is such sadness in that film and a longing not just for romantic love but to belong and have a home. Both the characters expressed that. The strange thing was that in the 40s section of it, the two main characters are old men. They're in their seventies. In a way, I could see my grandfather as an old man in them and that was what made the film so extraordinary. It was very prescient about what he was going to become and the kind of loneliness he had in his life. Theo in the film is someone who has been very proud of his country, but with the rise of Hitler, he doesn't want to be a part of it any more. He has left and come to Britain. He is a refugee who has arrived with nothing. He is treated like an enemy. There was a boldness in that. Who would have thought during the war making a pure German character the centre of the film. That was one of the reasons the film was so controversial at the time, but it is indicative of my grandfather and Michael Powell's humanism. Theo is a man who is living in a boarding house, one expects. He has no money. He is reliant on the generosity of others. He is rather shabby. He wants to belong to Britain, but he knows he never can. That was how my grandfather felt. I remember him telling me that the greatest man of the [20th] century was Winston Churchill. There was no question of that. He was an absolute God. When he upset Churchill with *Colonel Blimp*, he was absolutely devastated. You can't guess what a blow it was to him personally when Churchill turned around and attacked the film. He wanted his approval more than anybody else on earth. I remember him telling me that he queued for eight hours in the rain after Churchill died to pay his last respects.

Suddenly, the film had this great personal resonance for me. That was what led me to writing my book about him.

He died shortly thereafter. I left university. It was a time of huge unemployment. I wanted to work in journalism. I worked for a while in publishing. I never thought of being involved in film. I wanted to do some writing of one sort or another. I thought – I don't have a job, nobody else is going to write a biography of him, and I had had this connection with him in the last years of his life, so I'll do it. I set off writing his biography. That came very directly out of the experience of watching that movie. Then, out of writing that book, my interest in film grew. An interest developed in film history and in learning about film. I had made some small documentaries. The first longer film I made was about him. In a fairly cynical way, the book was my priority. I didn't have money to go to Eastern Europe to do the research I needed to do there. It was through getting some money from Channel 4 to make the documentary that I had some money to go. I got to make a documentary that I felt very bad about. It's not a very good documentary. I watched it not long ago – it was put on a French DVD. I felt it was a real missed opportunity. I appeared in it, which is cringeable. It was the right way to do it but I didn't quite know what I was doing and so it doesn't really work as a film. But I started to think that film was an interesting place to go. I realised that writing was fucking hard and there was no money in it.

I don't think there is any relation at all between my films and my grandfather's films. The influence is purely in the sense that he made it accessible to make a film. You don't have to have had a special experience in your life or to be a special person to make films. You can make films from what you know and what you are interested in.

I think my grandfather would have disliked my documentaries. I don't think they have that humanist quality his films have. He would have found them rather dark. "

Paul Schrader

Pickpocket

(Robert Bresson, 1959)

Paul Schrader is an intense and restless figure. Born in 1946 in Grand Rapids, Michigan, to Calvinist parents, he grew up in an environment where watching films was frowned on. He tells stories about how his mother impressed on him the idea that hell was for real. 'We believed in a very real hell and a very real evil. My mother took my hand once and stabbed me with a needle. I went ow! She said to me, you know how that felt, when the needle hit your thumb? Well, hell is like that all the time.'

His family may have been religious but that did not stop them from being obsessed by hunting. His uncles all had guns and hunting dogs. As a writer and film-maker, Schrader has been a chronicler of loneliness and violence. As he has written, he is drawn to 'a certain character: a person, usually male, who drifts on the edge of urban society, always peeping, looking into the lives of others. He'd like to have a life of his own but doesn't know how to get one.'

His fascination with cinema began in unlikely circumstances. As a teenager, he saw the Elvis Presley vehicle *Wild in the Country* (1961), and was bowled over by its vibrancy and eroticism. Schrader was a student at Calvin College, a seminary in Michigan. Partly because of the austerity of his family and educational background, he began to rebel. 'I became interested in movies because they were not allowed,' he once said.

When I interview him in a hotel in London, he is finishing the post-production on *The Walker* (2007). This follows on from *Taxi Driver* (1976), *American Gigolo* (1980) and *Light Sleeper* (1992) as another of his closely focused studies of alienation. What makes Schrader unique is that his work seems quintessentially American but is also informed by European film and literature. He is a chronicler of US street life, pornography and corruption but also someone who looks to Sartre and to French film-maker Robert Bresson, whose film *Pickpocket* provided him with his greatest epiphany.

His work often pulls in competing directions. On the one hand, he is fascinated by decadence and corruption. His New Orleans remake of *Cat People* (1982) was shot in lush colour and had a strong melodramatic undertow. On the other hand, he is drawn to characters with a Jesuit-like self-discipline. In *Mishima* (1985), his biopic of the Japanese writer Yukio Mishima, he celebrated a figure who was not only an intellectual but someone obsessed with physical discipline and the cult of the body. On the face of it, the Japan of *Mishima* was a long way removed from the terrain of his other films. However, Schrader protagonists from Travis Bickle (Robert De Niro) in *Taxi Driver*, the Vietnam vet getting himself in shape to be a vigilante and clear the sidewalks of scum and lowlife, to the narcissistic but extraordinarily disciplined male prostitute Julian Kaye (Richard Gere) in *American Gigolo* were similarly driven and self-obsessed figures.

As a former film critic who once wrote a book called *Transcendental Style in Film: Ozu, Bresson, Dreyer*, Schrader has an immense knowledge of film history and film theory. However, he is also a pragmatic film-maker. His admiration for *Pickpocket* was not only rooted in his awe at Bresson's treatment of such themes as love, alienation and bad faith but also in the film's craftsmanship. He saw in it a model that he could emulate when it came to making his own films about 'a man alone'.

Paul Schrader:

" In 1969, I was a reviewer for the *LA Free Press*. I was a protégé of Pauline Kael and very much set on becoming a film critic. *Pickpocket* was finally released in Los Angeles, ten years after the fact. It was shown at the big arthouse theatre in Los Angeles. I saw it and I was extraordinarily impressed in a way that it took me a while to figure out why. Rather than write a single review, I wrote about it for two weeks running. Even though my reviews were long, I couldn't fit everything I had to say in the space for one review. Out of that came the desire to write the book on transcendental style. More importantly, I saw a kind of film that I not only liked but I knew how to make – I knew I could make. This was a kind of existential character drama about a single charac-ter who is in every scene and who drifts around, peeping in on the world, who is a solitary man, who lives in a spare room and who is slowly undergoing a transformation. Now, I never have tried nor would I ever try to make a film as austere as Bresson did. That is a very specialised kind of talent and I am not that kind of film-maker. You don't com-pete in that territory unless it's the only way you know how to make films. You can't copy Bresson. But I have been

making that sort of film ever since with variations and deviances. The one I am just finishing [*The Walker*] is again about a character who lives alone, who is in every scene, who moves in and out of a world and who is slowly going through a transformation that he is not fully aware of.

For me, that epiphany was rather sharp. When I saw films by Bergman and Antonioni, I saw great films – films that made me want to write about films and be involved in the film world but I never saw anything that I thought I should be doing or I could be doing. I think that I started thinking about maybe writing a script myself after seeing *Pickpocket*. That's when my mind started shifting to maybe not being a critic. I knew I could make a film like that, not a Bressonian film but a film of that nature. I knew how to make that film. I understood that. *Taxi Driver*, of course, was that kind of film. The script [I had written] before that, called 'Pipeliner', was a kind of attempt to make a more Bressonian kind of script. I finished the script but it never went anywhere. It took place back in Michigan. It was about a guy who worked on a pipeliner, a job I used to have. It was a fellow who was dying who thought he could get away with anything and he ended up screwing around, screwing other people's wives, and it turns out in the end that he is not dying at all. That was very much a young man's script. By the time I wrote *Taxi Driver*, I knew the mistakes you can make. There was a preciousness about that script that you often have in a first script. Even though I called *Taxi Driver* my first script.

Sitting there at that cinema as a reviewer watching *Pickpocket* in the afternoon was, I guess, my moment of epiphany. Bang! It was instant. I went to the theatre and I had to file a review. I realised there was a bridge here between the world I grew up in and the world I am now living in. I thought they were two separate islands. I just saw somebody who constructed a bridge across.

I had [already] seen Bresson's *Diary of a Country Priest* and I was a big fan of it, but it didn't affect me in that Dostoevskian way that *Pickpocket* did. Maybe that was because *Pickpocket* was about criminal behaviour rather than Christian behaviour.

Pauline Kael once described him [Bresson] to me as a thin little man who fucked thin little boys in thin little rooms. [Laughs.] Even though she was a fan of *Country Priest*, he definitely wasn't her kind of guy.

For me, Bresson's career progresses in three phases. He begins with the comedy of manners. He then moves into this central phase where he progressively secularises the protagonists. It begins with a priest, becomes a criminal, then it becomes a war prisoner, then it becomes a young girl and finally it becomes a donkey. When you start trying to canonise or sanctify a donkey, you're pretty much pushing the end of that particular line of thought. Then he moved into colour and those films didn't have the same attraction for me.

I did meet him. We [Bresson and I] had been corresponding because I had been writing a book. He communicated with me. He didn't necessarily agree with what I thought about his work. Like most sensible film-makers or artists with those people who are gushing over you, you think they're a little bit silly. It's nice to hear somebody say how great you are but, you know, you're smart enough not to believe them. I was passing through Paris to go to Cannes [where *Taxi Driver* was screening]. I interviewed Bresson. It was a very peculiar interview. I ask a series of questions and he gives a series of answers but they're not really connected. He is very evasive. He gave very, very few interviews anyway. He only gave this

Pickpocket

Wild in the
Country (Philip
Dunne, 1961)

SCREEN EPIPHANIES

interview because we had been corresponding. It wasn't a disappointment to me, because if you look at his work, you have an idea what kind of cat this is. You don't really expect Jean Renoir. I had been going up to Renoir's house. I knew him. He was the opposite. He [Renoir] was just the soul of life itself. People would come over to Renoir's house on Saturday. I was invited there a number of times. Something he liked to do was to grab me, walk me over to someone and say this is Paul Schrader, he's a wonderful young critic, he's the critic who thinks Robert Bresson is a better film-maker than I am. Then he would walk off.

Last year, Criterion came out with a DVD of *Pickpocket*. I came out with an introduction to it. I watched the film again and gave it a lot of thought. I know all the elements that make it – a mixture of close-up fetishism and laconic blows, music coming in at the wrong time. There are a lot of things he does I would never want to do, like using non-actors. I like actors. I like the emotions they bring. Bresson didn't. Bresson was all about pushing you away so far that you finally reached out and grabbed it.

Boy, that's a tough act to pull. I was interested in how you can make a film about one person over and over again – how you can do a monocular film.

When I was growing up, films were not allowed. I didn't feel terribly deprived because I didn't know anybody who saw movies. It wasn't like everybody was talking about movies except me. Seeing *Wild in the Country* with Elvis Presley was an epiphany in the way that getting drunk was. You suddenly realised that there was a bigger world and a lot more fun out there than you knew about, but it wasn't an epiphany in terms of how to challenge your life. Those kind of things that happen when you first fall in love or get a job or do anything, they define you. When you talk about a film epiphany – something that defined what you were going to do not only as a critic but as a writer and a director – it all started with watching that film. I do watch the Bressons from time to time just to remind myself of how and why I got interested in making films.

Were there other epiphanies? If you start talking about multiple epiphanies, the word starts losing its meaning. It becomes 'epiphany of the week'. **”**

Anthony Minghella

The Blue Angel

(Josef von Sternberg, 1930)

Anthony Minghella was one of the first interviews completed for this book. I spoke to him at his offices in Hampstead not much more than a year before his death in March 2008. He was a generous and thoughtful interviewee, prepared to give up most of his afternoon despite his frantically busy schedule. Alongside his own career as film director, Minghella was also active as a producer (he was a partner with Sydney Pollack in Mirage) and as an opera director. At the time of the interview, he was also still Chairman of the British Film Institute.

As a director, Minghella dealt in big themes and big emotions. Unlike many other British directors of his generation, he wasn't scared of epic cinema: of tackling big literary novels and dealing head-on, and without irony, with intense emotion. In a way, he was a throwback. Not since David Lean had a British director been working on such a huge canvas.

His international breakthrough, *The English Patient* (1996), had a tortuous history, eventually being 'rescued' by Miramax. But this only seemed to add to its mythic status. Minghella proved that he was a craftsman, capable of staging big set-pieces and working with small armies of extras, but he was equally adept at capturing emotion in scenes between just two actors. He made an international star out of Ralph Fiennes and also elicited one of Kristin Scott-Thomas's very best performances.

Minghella's debut feature, *Truly, Madly, Deeply* (1990, made for BBC TV but released as a film), starred Juliet Stevenson as a woman haunted by her former lover Alan Rickman. The film had some overlaps with the Hollywood tearjerker *Ghost* (1990), but Stevenson and Rickman brought a delicacy and subtlety that wasn't present in the work of Patrick Swayze and Demi Moore.

As if to show that he was a miniaturist as well as a purveyor of epic widescreen cinema, Minghella made an excellent screen adaptation of Samuel Beckett's *Play*. Essentially comprising of just three talking heads, the film still had the impact and intelligence – and the clarity – of his more conventional films. There were magnificent moments in *Cold Mountain* (2003), notably an early battle sequence on a scale that rekindled memories of Cecil B. DeMille and D. W. Griffith, and some fine acting, particularly from Nicole Kidman. *The Talented Mr. Ripley* (1999), meanwhile, was a top-notch thriller with real psychological depth, in which Minghella managed to make us care about the psychopathic but ingenuous Tom Ripley despite his misdeeds. It ranks alongside Alfred Hitchcock's *Strangers on a Train* (1951) and Wim Wenders's *The American Friend* (1977) as one of the best Patricia Highsmith adaptations.

Minghella had graduated from the University of Hull in 1975 with a First Class Honours degree in English Drama, and returned to Hull to lecture for seven years while studying for his doctorate. During the 1980s, he served a stint as a TV script editor on *Grange Hill*, and subsequently worked as a script editor and writer for various television series, including *EastEnders*. He wrote episodes of *Inspector Morse* and won plaudits for his 1986 play, *Made in Bangkok*. A foray to Hollywood to make the romantic comedy *Mr Wonderful* (1993) was not especially successful. Minghella's real breakthrough came with *The English Patient*. His triumph was to take Michael Ondaatje's award-winning but very complex and literary novel and to turn it into a big-screen epic romance with the sweep of an old David Lean movie.

Anthony Minghella:

"There is a film I would like to talk about but my memory of it is so opaque. The film that really made me engage with the idea of what a film could be or could do was *The Blue Angel*. I didn't see it at the cinema. I saw it on the television on a night when my parents had gone out, which was a very rare occasion because they worked. They had a café on the Isle of Wight which was open most of the time, most of the year. It was open 365 days a year. It was open from morning to night. At a certain point, my nights became my own because my parents weren't there to supervise me. They apparently came home one evening and found me completely devastated. It transpired that I had been watching *The Blue Angel*. I can't date it but I certainly wasn't ten. I must have been seven, eight or nine. My memory is of this appalling humiliation of a teacher in love with a cabaret performer – Marlene Dietrich. It begins with an extremely curmudgeonly, rather rigid and puritanical schoolteacher who finds out some of his pupils have been visiting the cabaret. He then pursues them and gets sucked into the life of this cabaret. When he marries Marlene Dietrich, he is then forced to perform in this cabaret. There is a sequence in which he is humiliated by Dietrich and has to go on stage in his clown's make-up. This is all forty years ago or more that I saw this film. I can only remember glimpses. Shards of this film remain in my mind. What I remember was that it was the first time a piece of fiction had had such a devastating emotional effect on me. A lot of children remember seeing cartoons, *Pinocchio* or *Bambi* or something that breaks their heart. I remember seeing *The Blue Angel* and it breaking my heart. It was the first time I realised there was an adult world – that adults could damage each other or destroy each other emotionally. It might have fed into a whole series of epiphanies about my own upbringing. I was living in a family where my grandparents had separated in quite complex circumstances. Perhaps it resonated with some elements of that, to do with simply how love can be a rupturing and damaging emotion as well as a healing one. Also, to see somebody who is in an authority position made so small, so diminished, by the feeling of having no control.

When I was a teenager, I was very much aware of the impact of film fiction. I had seen a lot of it and I had had access to the cinema. Where I grew up, our cafeteria was adjacent to a cinema.

The Blue Angel

The projectionist rented a room in our building. There was always complete, free and unfettered access to the projection room. When I first decorated a space that was mine, it was decorated from floor to ceiling with film posters. They were probably absolutely unique items but I didn't realise. They were like wallpaper. There were lots of strange B-movie titles but I remember wallpapering more than I remember what was on them. I think I had a couple of David Lean posters. I seem to remember a picture of Robert Mitchum. And I certainly seem to remember an Egyptian scene – *King's Solomon's Mines* perhaps. But they weren't selected with any kind of discerning aesthetics. They were simply ways of wallpapering my walls that made my room look very quirky. Most of my day was taken up with working for my parents. When we weren't at school, we worked in the café. One of my earliest movie experiences was selling ice cream in the cinema, carrying a crate of tubs around in the intermission of the films. I don't have a romantic or nostalgic memory at all of cinema. I have never resented my childhood. It was a blessed childhood in the sense that I had a wonderful family. I don't resent the lack of cultural information I had as a child. It made me very enquiring and

curious. I've always imagined that you find your culture rather than receiving it on a plate. With my own children, they've tried to discover their own maps because the map in front of them is so defined. Sometimes the weight of a cultural hegemony you experience if you live in a home with books and music and arts can be as tyrannising as having no pointers and no references. I had my own mini *Cinema Paradiso* experience of watching movies through the projection hall. When I realised that fiction had teeth and claws and tears, it was this experience with *Blue Angel*. I can remember where I was sitting – on the floor of my parents' living room.

There are these rites of passage, these disturbances that lace together to push you into adulthood. I suppose *The Blue Angel* was one of those early disturbances. That is how I view it. There are these fissures in the steady progress from childhood to adulthood. Those fissures determine what kind of adult you will be. In particular, what I remember is watching it by myself. That made it much harder to bear. I think if I had watched it with somebody else, maybe with adults, I would have had some mediation between it and me. But because it was an entirely unmediated experience, because it was undiluted, I remember my parents coming home and finding me in a place where I was so overwhelmed. I was in floods of tears. I tried to explain what had upset me. It was a subtitled movie. I have a strange theory – the engagement with subtitles is not a distraction but has an oddly intensifying characteristic. You're using the reading brain as well as the seeing brain. When they're both engaged, the effect can be more powerful because you're dealing with something where you're having to actively decode events. It's a very curious thing. Some of my favourite movies, some of the most piercing movies, have been when I have had to read what is being said as well as listen and watch.

Marlene Dietrich's character was exotic and unknowable. The existence of an erotic life was again another secret to me. It was clearly on display in that film. When I talk about these fissures, that probably is the beginning of a sense there is an erotic life. I was an extremely avid reader as a child in a way that as a teenager I wasn't at all. From the ages of five to ten, I was addicted to reading. I would read under the covers with a torch. I read widely and wildly, with no control or compass. My parents didn't have any books at all. We had not a shelf of books. My parents

The Blue Angel

weren't able to monitor us because they were working all the time. So we found books from the library, but also books lying around to pick up. We had no sense of what was an adult's book. I remember reading *The Nun's Story* aged seven or eight years old, being absolutely fascinated. That has its own indications of an erotic life that runs counter to a religious life. One of the imprimaturs of my childhood was religion because my parents were incredibly religious. My grandmother was religious. We went to church a lot. We were Roman Catholics. I was taught by nuns until I was eighteen – so there was a very strong sense of the catechism and then this cultural offering [*The Blue Angel*] was in diametrical relationship to that. It was about all the flip side to those assertions. I was going to school in the 60s, when there were convulsions in the world of education. *If …. .* had an enormous impact when I was thirteen or fourteen. We all went to see that film and thought it was the holy grail. The system – one type of culture of post-war assertion of the status quo and an unending vision of England and Britannia – was all fragmenting. It was a fascinating time to be growing up.

The festivals came. I saw a documentary (about the Isle of Wight Festival)

MINGHELLA / *The Blue Angel*

recently. When you look at it, it looks as if modern England came to England on a ferry. It was like time travel. If you see this documentary, you have got one culture which is so hermetic and so certain and so smug and it is invaded literally by boats of the 'modern' – people in Afghan coats. It was a modern with a sell-by date that would soon evaporate but it had such a seismic impact on a small island which, as somebody said, was two hours and twenty years from London. If you could imagine that in 1960, it was more like 1940. To be caught in the middle of that collision was a fascinating experience – a very important and indelible one in terms of having an opinion about the relationship between stable institutions and what the inner life is – the way that the inner life is struggling and convulsing and fighting to make sense of the world. Maybe in the heart of *The Blue Angel*, there is a school environment that comes undone – where the teacher comes undone, where the kids come undone and where the status quo is capsized. Maybe that is why the film had such an impact on me. I could have talked about *I vitelloni* but if you're talking about a screen epiphany, that was the true epiphany. I haven't seen it again and that is perhaps why it has such totemic value. I remember just these four or five images – I remember a classroom, I remember a boy walking along a street toward a club, I remember the guy going into the club for the first time and being mesmerised by Marlene Dietrich. I remember her outfit. I remember the look of him with this make-up and the clown's outfit and some sort of laugh that turns into a terrible howl. That basically is all I can remember but in there is a whole series of very important archetypal reactions and encounters that haven't left me. Tonally, it had an impact on me when I started writing and I realised that the way I wanted to write didn't observe the held, rather cool temperatures of British writing. I am much more attracted to the whirlpool of feeling and the collisions of tone that European cinema seems more comfortable with.

I was very much into painting and drawing. Art and music had much more impact on me because I could do both of those things. I had a piano at home and a bass guitar. My friends played with us. We drew and painted and we all hung out with the art department and smoked cigarettes and listened to jazz. There was a whole developed culture which I had access to. That community of people felt dislocated from the mainland. There was a different place called

The Blue Angel

England. We didn't live there but imagined what it would be like. It's four miles away. For 90 per cent of the year, you can stand on the shore and you could be looking on the other side of the street. And yet it has another set of values. It is the unknown. We all imagined a world that we would get on the ferry and go off to and find ourselves. The island was so small, so eccentric and so idiosyncratic. There was this insularity that if you shook hands with somebody at one end of the street, somebody had written about it at the other end of the street. There was a sense that there was nowhere to go because it was all being reported and patrolled. You would imagine a world where you would have an opportunity for personal liberty.

I didn't ever think of myself as a storyteller when I was a teenager. I wanted to be a songwriter, but I didn't think of myself as being able to. I did know people who made music. I knew people at school who were making music. There was a channel that I could see of performing in clubs and in cafés and restaurants and bars. I had various jobs playing the piano in bars and in restaurants. The Isle of Wight had a big summer entertainment scene. There was a big folk club circuit there. There were the Isle of Wight festivals which meant as a young teenager, music was very viable. People were doing it who I knew. But I had never seen anyone with a camera. I had no sense of how that happened. Although I lived next to a cinema, it took me a long time to [understand how films were made]. A cultural matrix which said that books are written as well as read is a very specific world. I didn't know where that world was. I assumed that books arrived titled and made and that there was no one anywhere struggling to write a book or make a film or think about what kind of film could be made. We were just receivers of culture. We were lucky if we ever saw any. I don't mean this was some kind of privation. It was simply a way that you experienced culture merely as product. There was no process that you were admitted to. It was only when I became a student that I realised there was process. Philip Larkin was our librarian. I realised that the guy who made these books also walked around and did his shopping. He must have therefore sat down at some point and written these poems. It started to occur to me to make a deconstruction of the finished article. Then, from that to the idea that a movie was made and that somebody had an idea of a script and drew pictures. By the time I graduated, I had started trying to make films myself. It was quite a long journey of penetrating culture – a sense of simply coming to terms with the fact that culture didn't just exist – it was created and processed.

I think that the entitlement that you require to have to think you can tell somebody a story, that was something that didn't even occur to me. I didn't think I would ever be in the position to have the authority to tell a story. I was in a culture and a social territory that wasn't empowered in any shape or form. My parents were immigrants. We were people who worked in cafés and sold ice cream, not people who had the right to talk about their lives in public or to dramatise them or to fictionalise them or to give pleasure from our rehearsal of them. It never occurred to me that I might be in a place where I could be a film-maker. It never occurred to me until I went to university that ordinary people could have access to the complex club that is the world of cinema.

When I was in my third year of university, I was writing music. I wanted to do something with theatre. I started to write a musical. I wanted to submit some music but the department wouldn't allow it. So I thought I would write some text to lace these songs together. I

adapted a short story. There was a sequence I wanted to be an exterior sequence. I didn't know how to do it but I thought I would film it. The department had a camera, a Bolex. So I went out and shot a little sequence in the park and had a lot of fun with it. I've often thought that for all of us, opportunity is everything and it is not an accident we turn out the way we turn out. I went to a brand new department that had extraordinary facilities including a Steenbeck and a film camera the students could have access to. The fact of the matter is that I shot it because I could. I had the camera for a day and I could use it and the cutting room for a day. If there had been no Steenbeck or no camera, I would have thought of some other way of fixing this hole in my little idea. Having done that short scene, I thought I would make a full-length movie and so I borrowed some money. What's interesting to me is the odd galvanising of immigrant parents. My parents resent being called immigrants because my mother was born in England and my father came to England so young. But there is this drive and determination of people who settle in other countries.

When I wanted to make this musical piece for my degree, there was no piano available in the department and we couldn't afford to rent one. I played the piano for forty-eight hours and got sponsored and we got a Bechstein, and so I had a piano that I could play. When it came to making this film, there was no money in the department to help me make a film and so I went out and borrowed money. It took me nine years, with some other friends who helped me, to pay off the loan. I just wanted to make a movie. It was a catastrophic first attempt. It's in a drawer somewhere. But it was me learning the cruel parade of film-making – how much it takes of your resourcefulness and willpower to make a film but also how addictive and extraordinary it is.

The presence of a Bolex was very important, but this was still not real film-making. I had never met a real film-maker. My children met film-makers before they could speak, they met novelists, they met poets. I remember that when I was working on the *The English Patient* with Michael Ondaatje, my son was working on some opus – half novel, half film script – when he was six or seven. I remember him reading it out to Michael. I had never met a novelist until I was in my twenties.

The only ambition I had was to write, and everything else has turned up in front of me. I didn't go actively seeking to be a director or producer, but when I started directing, I felt like a man who had discovered that his hobby could be his job. All the things I like to do are allowed – I like to play music, to draw, to write; I was an academic for eight years and I love the world of the library; I like the interaction with other people and the requirement to be alone; I like working slowly, which film requires, and I like to plan; I love sound studios and music studios and darkrooms. There is no part of the film-making journey that doesn't interest me. When I stumbled into it, I found how well cast I was in terms of temperament. The thing I have discovered is that there is quite a sharp distinction between my instincts as a writer and my instincts as a film-maker. I have very small handwriting, really small handwriting. Oddly enough, that mirrors my interest as a writer. I love detail, minutiae, oblique inflections of character and personality. As a film-maker, nothing would make me happier than doing work with 1,500 extras and a big paintbrush. To feel like you have an enormous palette is a great pleasure and enormously rewarding. What is great about the movie world is that you are allowed and you are encouraged to flex between the epic and intimate.

A woman's face and the battlefield are the two essential images of the movie business. There is something about the movie close-up. *The Blue Angel* was probably the first time I saw a woman lit with erotic intent.

I am very hungry to continue to collide with arresting art and arresting culture. I think we all are, whether we make it or simply consume it. We're on the prowl, open-mouthed, for the food of culture. You're always an audience. All the people I know who make art and first and foremost audiences, because you can only make two or three pieces of art a year. You're much more frequently in the position of consuming culture than you are of creating it. I think we're innocent at the moment of consumption – but perhaps never as innocent as the boy sitting in front of the television watching *The Blue Angel*. "

Danny Boyle

Apocalypse Now

(Francis Ford Coppola, 1979)

When he gave his interview for this book, Danny Boyle was just about to start work on *Slumdog Millionaire* (2008), the Mumbai-set film that was to win him both Best Director and Best Picture Oscars. *Slumdog*, like the seemingly very different *Trainspotting* (1996, the film that made Boyle's international reputation), was characterised by its reckless energy. In Boyle movies, the protagonists don't sit around talking. He likes to show them full frame. Whether the setting is the backstreets of Leith or the slums of Mumbai, he eschews the clichés of social realism. The subject matter may be grim (poverty, drug addiction) but the tone of his films is always more celebratory than didactic. His colleagues testify to his focus and his enthusiasm.

Boyle has a very varied background. He is a working-class Mancunian who, on the one hand, is steeped in theatre (he worked for both Joint Stock and The Royal Court) and who, on the other, as a TV producer, came under the influence of the abrasive and brilliant British director Alan Clarke. There is seemingly nothing he won't try. He has made horror films (*28 Days Later ...*, 2002), sci-fi (*Sunshine*, 2007), noirish, Coen Bros.-style thrillers (*Shallow Grave*, 1994), US screwball comedies (*A Life Less Ordinary*, 1997), and kids' pictures (*Millions*, 2004).

At a time when other British film directors traded in chamber dramas or small-scale comedies and invariably struggled to shrug off the stifling influence of TV, Boyle was always ready to work on a bigger canvas. 'Realism is Britain's trademark in terms of television, drama and film. We've made this choice to dampen ourselves down so that sex and colours are not something to be celebrated,' he noted. 'If you go out on the street, we're such a small country architecturally and geographically that it is very difficult to create a sense of myth,' he said at the time of *Trainspotting*. It's a sentiment that Anthony Minghella (another, very different director interviewed in this book) shared.

Boyle remains a populist. He aims to reach as big an audience as he can, even if it sometimes means that the critics will come after him. His filmography is varied and uneven. His screwball romance *A Life Less Ordinary* seemed lightweight and conventional by comparison with *Trainspotting*. *The Beach* (2000) laboured under huge expectations thanks to the casting of Leonardo DiCaprio in his first role since *Titanic* (1997). It didn't fulfil these expectations. It began to seem that whereas Boyle could bring tremendous verve to smaller projects, his powers waned in relation to the size of the budget he was given. It was hard to recapture the irreverence and freewheeling gusto of *Trainspotting* when he was filming a studio-backed movie on location in Thailand with one of the biggest movie stars in the world. By contrast, when he worked with largely unknown actors on his post-apocalyptic zombie movie *28 Days Later ...*, he seemed liberated. He may have been ex-BBC and ex-Royal Court, but Boyle was not too snobbish to throw himself into making a genre film. Nor did he have any qualms about making a family film like *Millions*, the Frank Cottrell-Boyce-scripted yarn about kids stumbling on a bag containing hundreds of thousands of pounds that they only have a week to spend before the British currency switches to the Euro.

Showing his ability to tackle the most disparate projects, Boyle has also made the thoughtful, New Age sci-fi drama *Sunshine*, a brilliantly designed galactic epic that was clearly nodding in the direction of Kubrick's *2001: A Space Odyssey* (1968). Boyle is a paradox: a genial figure with no airs who nonetheless tries to push his collaborators in the same manic way that ego-driven directors like Werner Herzog and Francis Ford Coppola do.

Danny Boyle:

" I am a twin. I have a twin sister. We come from a very good working-class family. When we were about seven or eight, my dad took me to see *Battle of the Bulge* and my mum took my sister to see *The Sound of Music*. That gives you an insight into the gender upbringing. I don't remember anything about the film apart from a lot of tanks. That was my first experience of cinema. It was in Bury I think. I come from a town called Radcliffe, which is outside Manchester. It's a very small town and all the cinemas are closed.

In Bolton, another town near me, when I was about fourteen, me and my mates used to try to get into this porn cinema. It showed basically Danish porn. We didn't always get in but we got in sometimes. Then we got in to see *Clockwork Orange*. It was only out for about three weeks in Britain before all that trouble with the tramp, killings and all of that, and he [Stanley Kubrick] banned it. I was one of the few people who saw it on its original release. I got in to it. It was an X. That had an amazing effect on me. All I remember of it is the first half. I didn't remember any of the stuff that came back to haunt Alex but I could remember almost shot for shot all the stuff where Alex is transcendent and victorious. It is extraordinary to look back on it and realise that I didn't remember at all the moral of it. It was the excitement I remember of seeing this violence I suppose, and sex and style, really. That stuck with me, the style. I definitely used that style – that almost unbearable wide-angle style. It was fantastic. I remember me and this mate trying to get to see it. We would meet outside the cinema and we would plot how we would do it – which one of us would ask for tickets. We were only fourteen or fifteen. I would ask because I was the tallest and he would hang around trying to look grown-up.

I had picked up the idea that there were films I should like which were art films. I used to go to this cinema in Hulme in Manchester. It was a four-screen cinema. You could see art films there, everything, Truffaut, Pasolini, Jodorowsky … I had no idea what these films meant. I was there partly for the sex, which you could pretty much guarantee would be in the films, but also for the kudos of an art film. I don't quite know where I picked that up because there is no history of culture in my family at all. But I knew I was meant to like them. I didn't, to be honest.

Then I went to university. I did English and drama at Bangor in North

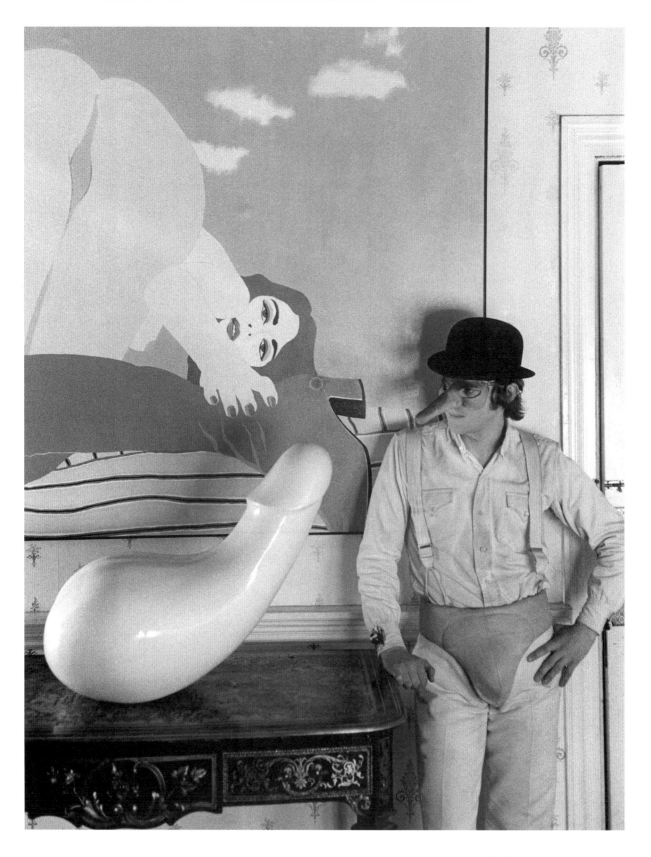

Wales. There was a film course and we were shown all these films and told why we should like them. Again, there were some of the films I had seen in Manchester. But I didn't like them very much. I didn't think they were very good, although I tried to convince myself that they were. I watched *Death in Venice* and all these films and I didn't really relate to them. I remember that feeling of callow youth where you try to convince yourself something is good when, in fact, there is no pleasure involved in it at all. When I look back at some of them, I think I was right – they weren't very good. They were overrated. Then I moved to London.

I had always wanted to be a film director since seeing *Clockwork Orange*, but it was in the same way that I wanted to be a train driver. It wasn't practical really. I never went about doing anything about it. I did plays at school and I directed assemblies on stage. Then I went to university and started doing drama. I started directing there properly but I was directing for theatre (not film).

When I came to London for a job in the theatre, I was living in a place in Fulham with some mates. They gave me a bedroom to stay in. I was an assistant stage manager, driving the truck, sweep-ing up and setting up the stages. They were an amazing company called Joint Stock Theatre Company. Outside the flat in Fulham, there was this huge bill-board. One day, this black poster went up with *Apocalypse Now* on it. I am sure I must have known something about it from *Time Out* or whatever. Anyway, I went to see it. That was the moment when everything suddenly made sense. I guess what it does it that it collides some of the elements of American mainstream cinema from the time and art. That was what Coppola had done in a way. What was interesting about it for me was that I was so transformed by it.

My dad came down to stay with me in London. I had moved to the East End, where I now live. I wanted to take him to see *Apocalypse Now*. The only place it was on was at the Prince Charles cinema. Then, unlike now, the Prince Charles cinema usually showed porn but they were showing *Apocalypse Now*. I took him to see it. Before the film began, there were all these trailers for porn. It was so embarrassing sitting there with my dad, watching these quite explicit group-sex orgy films. Then *Apocalypse Now* began and we sat there. What I remember was trying to persuade him how great it was. It was like trying to persuade him that Led Zeppelin and David Bowie were great artists and wanting him to come on board about it. But in fact I don't remember his response to it at all. Why that's weird is that he fought in the war. He was in the RAF. His friends were killed. He left the RAF because if you stayed in the RAF as what he was – which was a gunner – you basically got killed. You got paid a lot of money. You were very glamorous. You had the best uniform and the girls flocked around you but basically you died quite soon. So he left and transferred into the army, which was what a lot of guys did. It's typical of being that kind of age that I never really asked him what he thought of the film. I tried to convince him what a great film it was but he never spoke about it in that way.

There is something that haunts most directors, which is that we don't really do anything useful although we're thought of as being useful. He [my dad] fought in the war and contributed something and yet all I wanted him to do was watch Francis Ford Coppola's version of the war. It didn't undermine the film for me but it categorises film for me in a way. Film often runs in parallel with life and it feeds off it but I don't think it necessarily nurtures it. I don't think it necessarily contributes in the way we think it does. We, in our

Apocalypse Now

world, in our bubble that we work in, imagine that it does but I am not sure that it does.

It [*Apocalypse Now*] is a spectacle. What is extraordinary about it is that it rides two horses. It uses the spectacle and the war imagery and the violence in a still unmatched degree, which is the buzz you want as a young man watching it. And yet it is also clearly a warning. I watched it again yesterday. When you think of it now in the age of the executions put on the web, when you think of that end scene, when you think about the execution of innocent people and their beheading on the web for you to look at, then you think about the words about moral terror in the film. I was really disturbed by that. It's a boys' movie, boys wanting to be men. It is the ultimate boys' film. They always used to say that cinema was given over to boys and that after the 70s, cinema just became dominated by boys. I think that's not true. I think after the 70s, after *Apocalypse Now*, it became infantile. He [Coppola] says it wasn't *Apocalypse Now* that ended that era – it was Michael Cimino's film *Heaven's Gate*.

It just has an amazing voiceover. He [Coppola] got Michael Herr in to do the voiceover after he had shot the film. What I find very interesting about it –

and that differentiates it from Kubrick – is that there is no style. Why I think Coppola is the greatest there has been – greater in my mind than Martin Scorsese or Stanley Kubrick or even Nic Roeg, who is one of my personal favourites – is that there is no style. It is pure. I love style and I use style myself. But if you want to get to the absolute limit, there should be no style. You can spot a Nic Roeg film within seconds. You can spot a Stanley Kubrick film within seconds. Not because you are familiar with the material but because you can see the style straight away. You can't see any style in Coppola's films – there is no style. What you can see are these extraordinary scenarios. What is incredible about him is that everything is real. There is no CGI trickery with the helicopters. When the helicopter lands, you can see Martin Sheen is thinking, fuck, I hope this helicopter guy gets his landing right. It is a dedicated realism and a coverage of that realism. There is no style placed on it. It is recorded for you. The only moment of style you spot is the cut to the white square when the helicopters are coming. There is very little style in it as such.

Why the original version is better than the *Redux* is that clearly in the maelstrom of making it, when he was clearly going insane and he was haunted by what looked like a deadly, fateful press campaign saying the film had such problems, the decisions he made were all correct. When you look at the *Redux* version of *Apocalypse Now*, when you add romance or you add politics in the colonial scene, it doesn't add to it at all. The journey is almost without contact. There are none of those moments of contact or relief or sex or love or politics or civilised discussion or anything. There is nothing – just the boat and this narrowing river. I think why it is a great film is that he [Coppola] was as insane as the picture he was depicting. Notwithstanding that he had never been to war but in pure film terms, it is a credit to his genius that he can depict it like that, never having done it. I could go on and on about sequences in the film, obviously the Kilgore Valkyrie ride.

Do you remember the mangoes and tigers scene, when they go out looking for mangoes and eventually meet a tiger? It's blue – some blue steel grey, except the leaves, which are green. It is the most amazing piece of grading and cinematography. It's extraordinary.

It transcended the novella [by Conrad]. It feels so much like a part of the modern world. There are a couple of

Apocalypse Now

really shocking, cruel moments – the slaughter of the cow, and the puppy is treated quite badly at one point.

To be a film-maker, you can't behave like that to animals, but you have to lead – you have to be psychotic in your desire to do something. People always like the easy route. You have to push very hard to get something unusual, to get something different. To push it as hard as possible you have to be almost psychotic to do that, in a little mini-way. If you're shooting in the Philippines for a year through typhoons and heart attacks, then you are going to go as he [Coppola] did. There are some wonderful things in *Hearts of Darkness* [the film about *Apocalypse Now*]. When you are making a film, there is always a real low point. It's wonderful to remember this genius, this brilliant film-maker, say it [*Apocalypse Now*] is shit. It is worthless, it is fucking rubbish, I can't do it – that genuine self-terror you're not going to pull it off. That is always there. It is great to see someone as brilliant as him suffering it as well. You always imagine those guys do it so easily.

In my own films, I like taking groups of people and putting them in extreme circumstances. I think that is a wonderful premise – a pack of people under extraordinary pressure, whether it is self-imposed or territorial, and see what happens to them – see who explodes out of that.

There are sequences in *Apocalypse Now* that I can't work out how Coppola did. For example, when they're in the boat and they get fired on from the jungle and the tracer bullets come across. I couldn't work out how he did that! It's the real actors and the bullets pass by close. I think he substitutes impact. What you get in cinema now is impact – beheadings, limbs severing, knives going in. It's extraordinary the way the tolerance has grown for that in the last ten years. When we did *Trainspotting*, we weren't even allowed to show a needle going into the skin. We had to cut that to get a certificate. Now, you can plunge swords in – anything in a way. Coppola doesn't do any of that. You see very little of that. Instead, he does it through the scenario – the way he lulls you into a violent situation either by surprise or in hallucinogenic [sequences]. He doesn't do it like Spielberg does at the beginning of *Saving Private Ryan*, which is probably the only other film that has got close to the impact of *Apocalypse Now*. I'd be hard-pressed to think of a moment that you saw what you normally associate with savagery or screen violence. There is very little of it. You never see him hit Brando. Even when the commander of the boat gets a spear through him, you see the guy throw it and that's enough. You know it's coming. Then you hear it. And you see him – and he has the thing through him. The writer John Milius is a much more right-wing, military man – someone who approves of war, thinks war is a good thing. Clearly Coppola is battling that. The end that Milius originally wrote is that Willard and Brando got together and bombed the temple. I think Coppola threw it out and said it was trite and militaristic.

If I am honest, I've been haunted by *Apocalypse Now* for too long. When we made *The Beach*, *28 Days Later* ... and *Sunshine*, there has always been this Kurtz figure in them. I've never met Coppola. I saw him across a room once. That's it really. I'd have loved to have gone up to him and bowed down a bit.

Apocalypse Now was a complete, total influence. Being a film-maker [still] seemed very, very distant. The film industry was impossible to get into then, for someone like me. So I worked my way up in the theatre ... and the first image I ever committed to film was an upside-down head in *Shallow Grave*. **"**

Gurinder Chadha

Purab aur Pachhim

(Manoj Kumar, 1970)

The British film industry pays lip service to the idea of ethnic and gender diversity but it remains as true now as ever that the business is dominated by white, male film-makers. Gurinder Chadha has done more to challenge this status quo than any of her contemporaries.

In her 1989 TV film, *I'm British But ...*, she highlighted the complications of defining national identity for young British Asians. Her debut feature, *Bhaji on the Beach* (1992), about Asian women on a daytrip to Blackpool, likewise (and very playfully) explored the tensions between Asian culture and British working-class culture. The film was not well distributed and was therefore little seen. Chadha was determined that her subsequent work would reach as big an audience as possible. A decade later, with *Bend It Like Beckham* (2002), she enjoyed a runaway popular hit that transformed her into an A-list director. Since then, she has continued to make films that probe away at national and racial identity as intently as ever, but always with a populist touch.

Chadha was born in Kenya and came to Britain with her parents in the early 1960s. Her family settled in Southall, London, and later Chadha took a degree in development studies at East Anglia University in Norwich. Her route into film-making was circuitous. Embarking on her career as a journalist at the BBC, she gradually began to make documentaries about the British-Asian experience.

Her work is characterised by its humour and humanity. She is fascinated by family structures and by the conflict between classes, races and generations. At times, she seems to have a very British sensibility and to be attuned to British irony and deadpan humour. However, she is also capable of staging spectacular Bollywood-style set-pieces and of choreographing small armies of extras. She is populist and polemical by turns.

Gurinder Chadha:

"There was one real epiphany. That was in 1970, when an Indian film came out called *Purab aur Pachhim* directed by Manoj Kumar. *Purab aur Pachhim* means 'East or West'. It is the most fantastic Indian film because not only does it conform to a Bollywood tradition of songs and dances, it also has fantastic social and intellectual ambition. It was the first film that really tried to make sense of the British-Asian experience. The story starts during the Freedom Movement, before the independence of India. These two men are fighting for India's freedom. The British kill one of them. The other escapes. It's an 'oh, the Brits have been terrible to us' intro. Then, suddenly, it's 1947, India has won its independence and the British flag comes down all creaky in black and white, the Indian flag goes up and all of a sudden, the screen bursts into colour. You cut forward twenty or thirty years. The son of one of the freedom fighters is now the hero of the film. He is called Bharat [Manoj Kumar], which means 'motherland'. He is coming to England to study at Oxford. His dad died but the other freedom fighter survived and is now living in England with his two kids. Bharat comes to stay with him. He arrives with all his ambition in England.

As soon as he gets off the plane, he meets the other members of the man's family. The daughter has got peroxide hair, a miniskirt and high heels. The guy is wearing a flower-power tunic and trousers with a handlebar moustache. It's hysterical. You can watch it now and laugh at it. At the time, I was absolutely appalled. The whole film talks about how backward and fucked up kids growing up in England are. They have no sense of their Indian identity or sense of India's struggle against the British and they're losing themselves into the West. Bharat's job is to make them understand who they are. Of course, he does that. The hippy turns into a Hare Krishna-type person and the girl – he takes her to India. The film wasn't without wit and it was quite clever. It was prophetic in some ways. He [the director] knew what was coming but it was one of those films that had it so totally wrong that it was risible. On the other hand, there was nothing else out there. It was immensely watchable. It was an immensely important film for me.

As a young girl growing up in England, I wasn't even allowed to have my hair open. I used to have to have it in plaits. I remember when I was about fifteen, I had a huge fight with my mum just to let me have my hair in bunches.

Purab aur Pachhim

It was so taboo to have your hair open. Here was this girl with not only her hair open and poofed up but bleached and dyed and everything. And that miniskirt. Who the hell was allowed to wear miniskirts? We weren't allowed to do what this girl was doing. The film was a very extreme fantasy version of what this Indian guy thought was going to happen to girls in the West. But at the time, I was outraged by it because I thought people in India think we are like that and that I drink and I smoke and do things like that – and I don't. The reality is that when people emigrate, they become a lot more traditional rather than the opposite. There were more people behaving like that in India than there were here. The other reason I thought it was so hypocritical was that Bollywood actresses were dressed like that in Indian films as the norm during their song and dance numbers. I thought – how dare they accuse us of being like that? So what started happening with that film was my sense of injustice about how people portray me. That really has never left me.

The film was aimed primarily at India but was shown around the world. I am in touch with Manoj Kumar. I talked about him in a newspaper article and he called me up. He was very close to Indira Gandhi. People said he was being financed by her. His films were extremely nationalistic. They were all about rebuilding India and giving India a sense of pride and sense of itself post-independence. There would be a Bollywood movie going on and all of a sudden he'd cut to what was like a Russian montage of people in the fields with the harvest, people with sickles cutting the hay, India's green revolution, the flag. You know the famous Indian shot Raj Kapoor devised – the man and the woman standing back to back in the field. That iconic image of a couple together – the people of the land. *Purab aur Pachhim* was all about bigging up India, but at the same time, it was a fantastically innovative and original film to focus on the community here.

I must have been about eleven or twelve when I saw the film. For someone like me, the idea of [becoming a film-maker] doing that kind of job was never part of the equation. The idea of going into the arts in any shape or form was not part of my reality. My parents were very typical first-generation immigrants. My dad used to work for Barclays in Kenya. My grandfather had been quite wealthy. When he died, there were certain controversies over his estate. My father decided to come to

England to leave it all behind. When he tried to get a job at Barclays here, they laughed him out of the place. They said you must be joking. Do you think we're ever going to keep someone who looks like you, with a turban and a beard. He found it very hard to get a job. He had to cut his hair and [take off] his turban, and he got a job as a postman. The reason he took the job was that he didn't want to work at a factory. There were all these people who had BAs and MAs and they were still working in the rubber factory in Hayes. People were doing this unskilled labour. He thought being a postman was great. He was walking and he loved to walk. He was out getting exercise. And so that was the job he took. His whole working life for the next ten to twelve years was about him getting to a certain point and being denied a promotion which a white person would get above him. A Polish guy he trained then got a supervisor's position above him. He had this tremendous sense of injustice. He would move on to another job. He kept on moving jobs because of not really being able to get on. I remember when he was much older, going to the post office and seeing people from all over the world sitting behind the counter. I remember when he was young, he would say that was the prize job, to try to have a clerical position – to sit and serve behind the counter of the post office, that was like the gold mine of the job and they would never give it to an Indian. That stayed with him right till they gave him his pension. And my mum was also doing shifts in Wall's, the sausage factory in Southall. She did various factory jobs as well. Both my parents were working really hard in different kinds of shift work but within a year, had bought a house, a car and were doing very well, helping other people coming over. They would come and live with us, and my dad would help them get jobs or get a room or get their own place. They did a lot of that in the 60s.

The first job I remember ever really wanting to do was to be a long-distance lorry driver. We used to go on the motorway a lot to visit friends in Birmingham. I remember thinking how wonderful that would be – to get in a big truck like that and go anywhere you want on the open road. I loved going on the motorway and that was about the only job I really wanted, but that was to do with independence and breaking out and doing a job a girl was supposed not to do. When I was at school, there was a sense that girls shouldn't aspire to careers beyond teaching or nursing.

There was never any encouragement to think about writing or films. That was never part of the equation. My favourite subject was geography because that was the only course that gave me an international perspective on the world. I wanted to do development studies at university in Norwich. The career adviser said oh my goodness me, do a secretarial course, because then you've always got it. People like me are not supposed to get on. People like me are not the leaders of the country. We were not seen to be coming to much at that time.

My first sentence ever was 'I want' and then I would use the Punjabi verb for it. I think that's really interesting. My parents would speak Punjabi and then English as well. My first words were the combination of both. At school, there was this whole thing about 'you mustn't speak another language', you have to speak English. I always thought it so hypocritical. We had to learn French as well – and French was another language. As a child, I was so aware of all these hypocrisies. Later, I made a documentary about bilingual education. It completely changed. The prevailing idea now is that the more languages a child speaks, the more intellectual capacity they have for every other subject.

Kids are encouraged to speak two or three languages from a very young age. It just increases their brain mass. When I was growing up, it was seen as such a negative. It was as if we were seen as educationally backward and that our brains were not going to be able to compute two languages – the Indian language at home and the western language at school.

Every moment of my life has been a constant negotiation of different sides of me – and I would see it as a celebration. That's not to say there are no problems with that. Of course there are. But it's the problems that lead to the negotiations – that make it challenging but make us culturally alive as opposed to culturally dead.

When I was growing up in Southall, there were two cinemas. One was the Dominion cinema, which was a beautiful art deco building. My dad was a great lover of Indian films when he was young. He was forever singing the songs from Indian films but mainly from the 40s. *Mother India* was his favourite film. Although we didn't go that much with our parents, whenever relatives or friends came to visit us, they used to go to the cinema and we used to go with them. I saw quite a lot of Indian films as a child but not really understanding them, not really following the narratives. It is kind of impossible anyway, even as an adult, to follow some of those narratives because they are all over the place. But being fully aware of the experience of seeing people looking like you, that look like your mum and your dad and grandma or whatever, on screen and getting very emotional and crying when a son or a daughter does the wrong thing – those basic family messages of those films I understood. I remember it very clearly as a child. There was always a point where this older actress came on and would start crying and this Indian instrument, the sarangi, would accompany her tears. It was this wailing. It would be a wail, an emotional wail. Then you would have her tears. She would have this white sari on her head and she would be crying. I would start crying immediately. I didn't know what was going on in the scene but emotionally that pull was quite powerful. I remember feeling really stupid at the time but I couldn't help it. Then there was all the singing and dancing. We would just laugh at the clothes people were wearing, the funny hairstyles and how fat and ugly the men were.

But, just as exciting as the movies for me at that time was that during the interval, we would get cans of Coke, samosas and snacks. It was the going out of the house that was exciting. It was the ritual of going to the Indian cinema. The other thing that was great at the Dominion was that people would talk back at the screen. There was a lot of interaction. I loved that as well. I remember being in the cinema once and this couple on the screen were talking about where they were going to go on honeymoon. The woman says, 'let's go somewhere different, somewhere where there is a cool breeze blowing all the time', and someone in the audience said 'cut Southall!'. The cinema erupted with laughter. Things like that made it a great experience.

At the other end of Southall, there was another cinema, which is the beautiful art deco dragon one – it's now called the Himalaya Palace. I think it was called the Liberty when I was young. That was the English cinema and that was where I used to go to Saturday-morning pictures. That was the first cinema I ever went to. I remember vaguely being in my dad's arms. He took us to see *Song of the South*. I remember when the old guy comes on. He is singing and he has got the bluebirds on his shoulder. I remember absolutely freaking out. I couldn't understand the live man with the pretend birds and it just freaked me out totally. There would be lots of young kids sitting, eating crap, shouting at the screen and stuff. That was a whole other kid/gang experience. I saw *The Sound of Music* there and lots of musicals.

Finally, one experience that I go back to all the time and that was extremely precious was the Sunday- and Saturday-afternoon movies on TV. They were always on about 2 o'clock. It was on TV that I saw movies like *Up the Junction* and *Taste of Honey* and very gritty British social realist movies. I didn't know who Ken Loach was or any of that but what I really responded to when I look back is how culturally specific they were. Dora Bryan, for example, would pop up in these movies and her dialogue was the same in all of them. Her character was the same and so was the way she expressed herself. They were a genre and I thought they were immensely powerful because they were reflecting the world outside my door. You have the fakeness of Bollywood there and you have the Hollywood thing going on there, but what I saw on TV in the British movies was something very real and very palpable. I was fascinated. I didn't know what an abortion was. I shouldn't have been watching half that

stuff, I am sure. I remember watching *Up the Junction* and not knowing what that knitting-needle stuff was about. I didn't understand it. But what I got from that was that here was Dennis Waterman, who was obviously from the wrong side of the tracks. He was working class and the girl he fancied was very posh but it [their relationship] couldn't be. I could romantically understand that notion. It fascinated me as to why it couldn't be. What I was witnessing at first hand there were the class divisions in England. I was fully aware of cultural divisions but I was honing my perceptions of class during those movies.

For me, my experience with English families was obviously my friends in the street and their mums and dads or my school friends. We never visited English families' houses. My parents didn't have English friends. Even though we were living in England, I didn't have that interaction with English people in the same way. So, through these movies, I was learning and was fascinated to see how English people behaved. And then, of course, there were things happening in these films like when Rita Tushingham in *Taste of Honey* wants to go out with this black boy. I was, like, completely torn. I could completely

A Taste of Honey
(Tony Richardson,
1961)

understand why her family would be up in arms about it from a cultural point of view and from an Indian point of view. At the same time, there was another side of me that completely understood why that was unjust and wrong. So those films really provided the political backdrop of the social mores and reality of class and race in Britain. I was five or six, really young, but I remember saying in my head – this is how this society is, this is how I belong. That's very much what British society is about. It teaches you very early on where you belong. It's only now that I've seen *Up the Junction* and *Taste of Honey* as an adult that I am able to talk about them as films. At the time, they were like windows inside a world that I was familiar with but not familiar with. What I was doing was using the cinema in Southall to piece together my reality.

I went to Norwich, to the University of East Anglia and did development studies. While I was there, the riots broke out and Britain came of age. When I saw Brixton go up in flames and Bristol and Manchester and Liverpool, it was suddenly like – oh, my God, the country is changing. I was getting more and more politically aware. That's why I want to bring up *Cathy Come Home*. I remember sitting in the front room watching that film and being shocked and appalled at the injustice being meted out there. Again, I didn't understand it but it started to crystallise for me the sense of injustice of the society I was living in. I was very aware of how on *Z Cars* and *Softly, Softly*, programmes like that, criminals were always black. It was the beginning of me really assessing how the media works in terms of controlling images of us and the power of the media. I would never be precocious enough to mention that at the time but I was aware of how programmes like *Love Thy Neighbour* were wrong ... funny, but wrong, and *It Ain't Half Hot Mum*. I couldn't tell you why it was wrong but I knew it was wrong. To make matters worse, people of my parents' generation loved them and would laugh at them. *Mind Your Language* ... they would laugh at that. I'd say why are you laughing, it's not funny. I remember Michael Bates's character in *It Ain't Half Hot* all blacked up and my dad laughing because it was such a good impression. But I would say it was wrong. That schism happened where I was different to them. British television was teaching me the way society was going to be assessing me.

Then the riots happened. The country had a complete shock to the system and had to evaluate race and class and everything else in terms of what it means to be British. That's when I started thinking, shit, I know what I need to do – I need to get behind a camera. That was it for me. It wasn't about seeing some masterpiece film but about realising the power of the camera and how you can take someone who is seen as an outsider, an irritant, the shit of society, and turn that on its head. That's the first step to changing things. It wasn't film I aimed for. I thought I would get involved with the news and start telling the news properly – or more impartially. I did a course in journalism and trained to be a journalist. In that time, in London, it was the time of the GLC [the Greater London Council] and there were great political changes. You had *Film on 4* and *My Beautiful Laundrette*, *Letter to Brezhnev* and *Playing Away* by Horace Ové (which was the first film I saw that had a three-dimensional approach to black Britain in a way that was entertaining and moving). I remember seeing *Handsworth Songs*, which I really, really loved. It was something very British and very black (at that time, we all were black, if we were Asian, if we weren't white). It was so emotional. I saw it at the ICA. I remember being in floods of tears. Here was this very emotional feature documentary that trans-

ported me to a different place and made me think about the possibilities and the power of film to articulate the complexities of your own political and cultural make-up. I also liked *Looking for Langston*. That was a beautiful, elegiac, more intellectual film.

That's when I realised I wanted to try to start working on film. I had no experience or anything. I thought maybe I could do it through TV, move away from news and documentary. I was a researcher then on documentaries but I realised what was then important was to make films that featured people like me in them; I wanted them to be understood and appreciated by people like me. That became my division away from an intellectual kind of film-making to a more populist kind of film-making. I thought *My Beautiful Laundrette* was a really important film because it refused to be pigeon-holed into any category. That's what I liked about it. What I didn't like about it was the disparaging way it dealt with the Asian experience, but I think that was perfectly fair because that was Hanif Kureishi's experience as a mixed-race Pakistani boy, which was totally different to my experience.

I didn't want to make films for black people or just for people who were interested in race, experimental or arthouse film. I wanted to appeal to people like my cousins. I wanted to appeal to a wider society. When I did *I'm British But ...*, it was looking at cultural identity but not in a Stuart Hall, Paul Gilroy highly academic way, although I loved Gilroy's book *There Ain't No Black in the Union Jack*, which I read after I'd made the film.

I'm British But ... featured four Indian kids talking about whether they were British or not. It just so happened that one was from Northern Ireland, one was from Scotland, one from Wales and one was from England. When they came on the screen, you suddenly realised, huh? That's when I realised how you had to do it – don't put experts on the screen talking about it. Do it so you're confounding people all the time and confounding people's ideas all the time. That's the pattern of every film I make now. I take you in so you think you are seeing a nice 'we are the world' comedy. Then you start seeing people who you are not used to seeing on the screen. Then you start getting involved in their films emotionally. Then, before you know it, you're seeing the world from their point of view, not your point of view. Then I bring you into how you might be culpable for some of their problems. Then I put the political boot it. Then I cut back, saying you've got my point now but I still want you to go home happy. "

Mike Leigh

Room at the Top

(Jack Clayton, 1958)

When you go to interview Mike Leigh, you're shown up to a small apartment in a Soho building that appears to be inhabited primarily by prostitutes. You sit in a slightly shabby sitting room that makes few concessions to modernity. Leigh bristles and tuts at what he considers to be idiotic or poorly expressed questions. He is a spiky personality with a mordant sense of humour, but his somewhat curmudgeonly persona is belied by his generosity. He may think his interviewer's questions are moronic but he still answers them fully and amusingly. Leigh is also, undeniably, one of Britain's greatest living film-makers. *Naked* (1993), *Secrets and Lies* (1996), *Topsy-Turvy* (1999), *All or Nothing* (2002) and *Vera Drake* (2004) are all monumental achievements. They are far more varied than the caricatured vision of Leigh as a purveyor of realist dramas about class and social embarrassment might suggest.

Born in 1943 in Salford, Lancashire, Leigh was brought up in a Jewish immigrant family. It is a moot point whether he should be described as working class. His father was a doctor, and Leigh was a grammar-school boy who won a scholarship to the Royal Academy of Dramatic Art in 1960. Arguably, what has given him an edge over so many other British film-makers is the breadth of his experience. Leigh has often seemed to straddle two worlds. He is the northerner who made good in London, the RADA and art-school student who directs gritty social dramas, the humorist with the dark perspective, and the great film director who spent a good part of his career working in television. In the class-conscious world of British cinema, this meant that his achievements were slow to be recognised. It was only when *Naked* and *Secrets and Lies* won plaudits and awards in Cannes that the British film establishment began to take note. The irony is that his audience – at least in the UK – has diminished since the days when he was working in television. Back in the days before multi-channel TV fractured the audience, Leigh's TV work like *Nuts in May* (1976) and *Abigail's Party* (1977) would reach many millions. There was a seventeen-year gap between his debut feature, *Bleak Moments*, in 1971 and his second film, *High Hopes*, in 1988. He made no secret, though, of his desire to work on the big screen.

Like his near-contemporary Ken Loach, Leigh is an example of a British director who has enjoyed an extraordinary Indian summer. Financiers are willing to back his projects even though he rarely divulges details of his films in advance. He is, as he has put it himself, 'the guy with no script and no casting who can't tell you what the film is about'. His producer, the late Simon Channing-Williams, had an extraordinary ability to secure funding for films on the basis of Leigh's name alone.

Leigh brooks no creative interference in his work. He doesn't hold test screenings or allow front-office money to make suggestions. Leigh's films evolve in the process of being made. This doesn't mean that they're improvised and that he simply rolls the cameras and allows the actors free rein. His working method is disciplined and thorough, involving endless preparation and rehearsal. Even if there is no script in advance, his movies are as carefully crafted and conceived in their own way as those of even Alfred Hitchcock.

Mike Leigh:

"It is a rather simplistic and all too tidy journalistic idea that a film is the only film that is an epiphany. It's a nonsense, really. One goes through an endless cycle of cumulative experience. Certainly, my filmgoing life experience is defined in the first place by the fact that between 1943, when I was born, and 1960, when I left Manchester to come to London, I never saw a movie that wasn't in English. I saw loads and loads of films because there were little picture houses, so-called, everywhere. There were four-teen within walking distance from where I lived without going into central Manchester. There was a big Gaumont. Each cinema showed two films in the programme. At that time, there were independent cinemas showing prints of anything that was around and so you saw pre-war prints. And there were the news theatres. It was all cinema!

The diet on which I was reared was Hollywood and British movies. The only two films I ever saw that weren't in English were *Rififi* by Jules Dassin, which had a very long sequence in which no one speaks, and that hideous, revolting saccharine piece of crap, *Le Ballon rouge*, which was shown at schools.

If you're asking me about my film-going experience in the late 40s and through the 50s, I don't really draw a distinction between the British movies and the Hollywood movies. They all came dished up together. In many ways, it was the golden age of Hollywood. And you took for granted that many a British movie was about World War Two. World War Two hung in the recent air. I don't have any particular nostalgia for films like *Doctor in the House* and *Genevieve* but I do remember being taken by *Genevieve* for three things – the cars (I've always liked vehicles), the music by Larry Adler and an early prepubescent crush on Kay Kendall, who was very sexy. But it wasn't a great film. A lot of those British films were soppy. One knew soppiness when one saw it. They were bloody soppy, really. I did do that thing which Terence Davies recalls in *The Long Day Closes* which now would be completely unthinkable, when you go and stand outside a cinema and say to someone, will you take me in? If it was an A, when a kid had to be accompanied by an adult, you would hustle somebody, who would then take you in. Then you wouldn't see him again.

The major epiphany isn't a film. It's September 1960 in London. Suddenly I was blasted from here to eternity by the French cinema, the Italian cinema, the Russian cinema, the Japanese cinema,

the cinema of Satyajit Ray, etc. That was the epiphany in a way. It was a massive culture shock and immensely liberating. You spent years sitting in the National Film Theatre and one or two other venues just eating it up – consuming it, being influenced by all sorts of things.

You had the National Film Theatre. Then, there was something called The International Film Theatre in Westbourne Grove. That's where I remember seeing *Jules et Jim*. That was a traumatic experience because at that time I was deeply in love with someone who was in love with somebody else. It was a very emotional experience. There was the Academy in Oxford Street. There was the Cinephone at the top end of Oxford Street, which is now a cultural desert. I remember seeing *Divorce Italian Style* there with Marcello Mastroianni. There were cinemas in Tottenham Court Road that showed international cinema. Then, above all and remarkably, there was the Tolmer, in Tolmer Square (which has now disappeared). Somewhere between Warren Street and Euston Station was this ancient square, in the middle of which was a church which had become a cinema. I had a flat for many years nearby in Eversholt Street. The thing about the Tolmer was

that it remained for many years the cheapest cinema in Britain. You never knew what you would see there. It was crummy in the extreme, the projection was awful, there was a section where you did not sit because that was where the browncoats and tramps sat and they drenched the seats with piss, but they would show whatever they got their hands on, not always complete. I remember seeing the original version of *The Leopard*. God knows where they got that from. You would see all sorts of stuff there. It was a real gas. And it used to cost two shillings. There was also a cinema by Victoria Station that claimed to be the oldest cinema in Britain and that showed international cinema. Then there was the Baker Street Classic.

Another thing which must also be discussed in the same time frame is that in 1959 in Salford, at the local cinema, I saw *Room at the Top*. I have a great respect for Jack Clayton (the film's director, whom I actually knew a bit). When I think back on *Room at the Top*, it was not a great film. When you look at it, it still has pretty ropey, old-fashioned acting and ludicrous casting. The choice of Laurence Harvey! He is as northern and working class as Oscar Wilde himself. But at the time I saw it, at the age of sixteen or whatever, the epiphany was

Genevieve (Henry Cornelius, 1953)

watching and experiencing a film that was looking at the real world – which was the very world outside the cinema when I stepped out into the street.

Whether historically that film is regarded as part of the so-called British New Wave of Karel Reisz, Tony Richardson and company, I've got no idea. Those films followed and were going on in the period when I was discovering 'World Cinema'. The interesting thing about those films is that they absolutely look at provincial, urban working-class life. From a cinematic point of view, all of them were adaptations of novels and plays. I have no truck with the argument that says all the filmmakers were public school-educated and upper-middle-class guys making films about the working class. I have no problem with that. To me that is an irrelevance. Artists can do whatever they like. But what is interesting is that the most original and organic film that came out of that movement was not until 1968, when Lindsay Anderson made *If ....* . It's a far purer cinematic investigation of something than any of those earlier films because they were all adaptations. Curiously, one of the most successful of those films was *Tom Jones*, which wasn't a contemporary working-class piece.

A Taste of Honey begins with a bus ride. It was shot by Walter Lassally and it has lovely shots of Manchester and Salford. That resonated with me. That was very nice and succulent and imaginative and evocative.

For me, having grown up in a working-class world (albeit as a middle-class kid whose father was a doctor) and having sat in the movies from an early age, thinking 'wouldn't it be great if you could see a movie in which people were really like people are' (which has motivated me for the rest of time), seeing *Room at the Top* in 1959 was a kind of epiphany. Now, when you look at it, you think Wilfrid Lawson is ludicrously over the top and Donald Wolfit is doing a Shakespearian performance. And what the hell Simone Signoret is doing in that place, goodness only knows. Having said all that, the landscape, the texture, the filmic quality – which is separate from the acting and the characterisation – really did look at that world in a way that resonated with my young head.

I can mention a stack of films more important to me than *Room at the Top*. I don't want to walk away carrying a *Room at the Top* banner – I really don't. All that is important is that it had a quality of looking at the world that resonated with me because I was in that

Room at the Top

world. But it would not rank in any way, shape or form as one of the films that really influenced me.

I find it remarkable looking back at that point in my life that I didn't join or pursue the Manchester Film Society. I don't know why I didn't. I knew it was there. I suppose I was too busy doing other things. What is for sure is that growing up in what was in film terms an uninformed environment, I didn't know that the English tradition of looking at [working-class] life goes back to Humphrey Jennings and even beyond that. Retrospectively, you realise that the Ealing films in some way did do that. In a funny, elliptical way, they did look at the real world. Then, within a couple of years, when you get to the quality of *Il posto* and early Fellini and early Kurosawa and Ozu and all the rest of it, you discover this is a whole world. Then there was the *nouvelle vague* – particularly *Les Quatre cents coups*, *Jules et Jim*, *À bout de souffle* and *Vivre sa vie*. Their cinematic language and way of approaching the world in an organic way was very much epiphanous.

I had a copy of *Film and the Public* by Roger Manvell, which was part of Penguin Film Studies. So I knew about Eisenstein and I had seen stills but it still seemed to me [when I came to London] that I had stepped into a world of which, previously, I had known nothing. It's like art – in one sense, you discover things gradually, but actually, things suddenly being there can be a revelation. One thing was certain – I knew I wanted to make films.

Talking about one film as an epiphany is impossible. The whole experience was a continuous, evolving epiphany and a continuous, evolving inspiration. It is very hard to isolate a burgeoning, growing experience. Of course, in among the positive manifestations of this mass epiphany were some monumental negative epiphanies. I like Antonioni's earlier films, like *Il grido*; but later they became deeply tedious. Very boring indeed, and most of us heterosexual young guys only ever went to see them because we wanted to fuck Monica Vitti. His films went from bad to worse – *Deserto rosso* was the depth of arty, pretentious bollocks, utterly devoid of irony, and *Blow-Up* is one of the most irritating, silly films ever made.

How does one isolate one particular film? When I hit town in the middle of 1960, one of the first films that was being screened round Tottenham Court Road was John Cassavetes's *Shadows*. One new aspect was that the actors

LEIGH / *Room at the Top* 71

involved had improvised. That was an important inspiration. I think Cassavetes did some great stuff but he also did some not very good stuff. I am obviously very experienced in the whole business of actors improvising. What you actually get in many Cassavetes films is no more than actors playing themselves. It's not about characters other than the actors, which is very limiting. He made some films – particularly *The Killing of a Chinese Bookie* – that were great stuff.

One of the other things I remember from the summer of 1960 was walking up and down cinema queues with a girl-friend when people were waiting to see *Psycho* and telling everyone that the butler did it! **"**

Shadows (John Cassavetes, 1959)

Mike Hodges

Sweet Smell of Success

(Alexander Mackendrick, 1957)

In *Get Carter* (1971), his debut feature, Mike Hodges directed one of the best British crime thrillers of the 1970s: a noirish, Newcastle-set story riven through with that mix of violence, eroticism and gallows humour that you find in Robert Aldrich's movies. What made *Get Carter* even more impressive was its very English flavour. This wasn't one of those would-be hard-boiled British films in which the characters all speak with transatlantic accents. Hodges rooted the action very firmly in the north-east and was fully alert to all the tensions that characterised the Britain of the time: the great divide between the 'north' and the south-east, the still evident class divide and the ambivalent attitude toward women. He was helped by a blistering performance from Michael Caine as the London gangster who heads 'north'.

The *Get Carter* credit gives a curiously lopsided feel to Hodges's career. An early success, it was undervalued on its initial release, but remains the film for which he is most famous. Hodges struggled to trump it. As historian Andrew Spicer has noted, his 'spasmodic career as a director illustrates many of the besetting problems of the British film industry'. He had problems with producers, notably on *A Prayer for the Dying* (1987), his film about an IRA hitman, and disowned the cut that eventually appeared. Moreover, his films weren't always distributed effectively. His 1998 feature *Croupier* was shelved by FilmFour and given a tiny release by the British Film Institute before becoming a sleeper hit in the US and later re-released in Britain. Hodges has made comedies (*Morons from Outer Space*, 1985), sci-fi films (*Flash Gordon*, 1980), supernatural yarns (*Black Rainbow*, 1989) and several thrillers (among them *Pulp*, 1972, and *I'll Sleep When I'm Dead*, 2003). Even so, his career has been characterised by long hiatuses. He himself has joked that his CV has 'holes in it like Swiss cheese'.

Hodges excels in making probing, intelligent dramas about corruption, greed and violence. A former director for hard-hitting TV current affairs series *World in Action*, he has always been prepared to confront the seamier side of human nature in his fictional work too. His stubborn, uncompromising quality counted against him in negotiations with producers who didn't share his vision. However, after *Croupier* enjoyed its unlikely second lease of life, critics began to look at his work anew. *Get Carter* was remade so unsuccessfully by Sylvester Stallone that it alerted many to just how good the original had been. Hodges was the subject of retrospectives and magazine articles. His filmmaking may have been patchy and sporadic but he still seemed a far more original and arresting director than many of his contemporaries with much smoother career paths. This ex-accountant from Dorset had somehow transformed himself into a genuine English auteur.

Mike Hodges:

" I was brought up in the provinces in Salisbury. There were three cinemas there. As soon as I was allowed in, I started going to the cinema. All in all, there were about eight films a week you could see. Without exception, they were all English-speaking films. However, I was lucky in that my formative period was in one of the great eras of film-making, particularly in American and British cinema. In Britain, you had Powell and Pressburger, Lean, Reed and other good British film-makers as well. In America, you had Billy Wilder, Hitchcock, Welles and a whole range of great directors. In my early days, I never missed any musicals. I never missed any Doris Day films. I used to go and see films with specific actors, like Barry Fitzgerald. My mother was Catholic, so weirdly I followed actors who I thought might be Catholic. It was a very arbitrary process.

I worked in a chartered accountant's office. The cinema was a wonderful outlet from office life, which was pretty tedious.

My bible really in those days was *Picturegoer*, part masturbatory magazine with pin-ups but also there was a critic who wrote in it called Margaret Hinxman. She became my guide. She would lead me to all sorts of really interesting films. I saw darker films like *Double Indemnity*, *Ace in the Hole* and *Sunset Boulevard* when they came out. I saw *All about Eve*. I became drawn to the much darker, more serious side of cinema-making. These very astringent, tough films began to appeal to me. I knew nothing about film-making. It was like having a bath or turning a tap on – they [films] just were there. I had no idea of the complications or process of making films at all. In the main, people still don't. The material is just there for you to get lost in. Then along came this film *Sweet Smell of Success*. I didn't know who the director was. I just knew that it was an extraordinary film. I was completely bowled over by it. Whereas *Double Indemnity* was a story of sexual corruption, the films I began to see were about social issues and the exploitation of innocent people. *Sweet Smell* had an incredible impact on me. I had no idea it was made by a Scot [Alexander Mackendrick] until years afterward. The film was just extraordinary in terms of the storytelling. Clifford Odets had written the script. There was a great musical score by Elmore Bernstein. There were these two extraordinary performances from these two Hollywood actors who were pin-ups and who until that point had seemed cliché-driven.

Double Indemnity
(Billy WIlder,
1944)

SCREEN EPIPHANIES

Burt Lancaster came from the circus. Tony Curtis was just a pretty boy basically.

Lancaster plays this horrendous gossip columnist, J. J. Hunsecker, so most of the action takes place around New York's theatre district, Broadway. It was a seductive film because it was also very glamorous in a way. We [in Britain] had just come out of a war. We had rationing and everything but J. J. was eating a nice big steak. And J. J. had this weird relationship with his sister with sexual undertones. I hadn't come across incest before.

Lancaster was extraordinary in the film. He was going to do *Black Rainbow* for me, playing the father of Rosanna Arquette, the role that Jason Robards ended up doing. I had long conversations with him. He was very bright but a pretty terrifying man. I think Mackendrick had a rough time making *Sweet Smell*. I could believe that. Lancaster was one of the producers which must have made it tricky.

In those days, gossip columnists in the US were very big, very powerful. There were people like Hedda Hopper and Walter Winchel who could destroy stars however big they were. In the UK, we had gossip columns but they were nowhere near as ruthless. Hunsecker was this appalling man, being fed bits of information, bits of gossip by Tony Curtis (Sidney Falco). It was just mesmerising to watch. It was also that the film was so tough. It never let up. There wasn't a moment of sentimentality in it. For me, that was an important lesson. Prior to this 'epiphany', I wallowed in the sentimentality being dished up in the cinema. Now I did a volte-face. I wasn't interested in sentimentality any more. I couldn't watch a musical to save my life now – a Doris Day musical or anything like that. That moved on into my work. There is no sentimentality in my films. I fight against it at every possible turn.

I managed to make two films for television in the late 60s. One was called *Suspect* and one was called *Rumour*. Well, *Rumour* was about a gossip columnist. Although very different to *Sweet Smell of Success*, it was also ruthless and tough.

What is difficult for younger people to realise is that exposure to your influences were very brief. We didn't have the advantages of video or television. You'd see a film usually just once. We were lucky in that our influences were more fleeting.

I didn't have any contacts in the industry. It was a nepotistic business. Most of the crew were sons or daughters of other crew members. The directors (certainly in Britain) were upper middle class. It was an elitist group. Not that they weren't good but they tended to be ex-university, ex-public-school boys mostly. The chances of my ever becoming a film director seemed very small. I can still hardly believe it ever actually happened. I am still astonished I got to make any films at all. I dreamed about being a film director but had no idea what it entailed. I remember going to a bookshop when I first came to London once to see if I could find a book on film-making. There was one book. It was by Paul Rotha. Now you have whole bookshops devoted to films. The number of books on film has probably exceeded the number of films made in the past thirty years. It's bizarre. In those days it [film-making] was just an innocent dream for me. But I knew that if I did make films, *Sweet Smell of Success* was the kind of film I wanted to make.

In 1964 I worked on *World in Action*. I got the job through James Hill, another British director, who is now dead. He and I began to make a documentary on the Profumo scandal but that didn't work out. He asked if there was anything else I wanted to do. At the time Jessica Mitford's *The American Way of Death* had been published. I suggested we do a documentary about the equivalent commercialisation of funerals in this country. We went to Tim Hewitt, who ran *World in Action*, and he said yes. I wrote it and did the interviews and Jimmy directed it. Having done that, Hewitt said to me, do you want to come and work on *World in Action*? I said, are you kidding? It was a dream programme for me. I used to watch it every week and thought it just amazing.

Again, the chances of making a feature film were still a million to one, although obviously I was learning and beginning to mix in some sort of [film] circle. I had started in television by getting a menial job as a teleprompter operator, again through chance. I'd met the son of the *Daily Telegraph* motoring correspondent. He was a floor manager at Rediffusion. Commercial television had just started. I got the job, ten quid a week – I worked there for two years, went to every [TV] studio and also in film studios. I realised then that I could possibly make films myself. That job diffused the aura that surrounds film-making. Walking into a studio can be quite terrifying but I had begun to have dreams that I might one day direct.

There was a season of films at the Everyman which I went to. New American cinema that had come from

*Sweet Smell of
Success*

television. Paddy Chayevsky was one of the major figures featured. Among the films was *The Bachelor Party*, *A Man Is Ten Feet Tall* and *Marty*. I went to see them all. Again, they all were socially conscious films – films that touch you and change you. You came out different to the way you went in in terms of how you viewed life and society. They were realistic and unflinching. The first films I made were sourced by these films and by *Sweet Smell of Success*.

During my period on *World in Action*, I began to see the world, and particularly America and the UK, in a totally different perspective. You witnessed corruption everywhere you looked. The British were very hypocritical in those days. They thought their policemen were wonderful and that other countries – foreigners – were corrupt, and that nobody in Britain was corrupt. I knew this was not true. My introduction to America had really reinforced my view of *Sweet Smell of Success*. I did a programme in 1964, a profile of Barry Goldwater, the Republican Presidential nominee. I saw the Republicans at work in the Dallas Convention. I saw the ruthless side of American politics. Next I did a programme on the American United Automobile Workers and I met [union organisers] Victor and Walter Reuther. Victor lost one eye, shot out by G-men employed by Henry Ford. Similarly, his brother Walter had a withered arm. I had always thought that the British unions had a pretty bloody beginning but it was nothing like the Americans. The setting up of the American unions was just a bloodbath.

Then, I went to Vietnam. I saw the naivety of the Americans – that they couldn't possibly win and that their cause was ludicrous. That was all in the space of about twelve months. It was a very formative period for me. It began to confirm that if I ever did get to make films, what sort of films I would make. When I made *Get Carter*, apart from being a gangster film, it was about a corrupt city [Newcastle]. Not long afterwards, the city's Manager ended up in jail. National politicians were involved – it went all the way down to London. I'd walked into something. You could smell it there – you could smell the corruption.

It's a long time since *Sweet Smell of Success* but you still see the press being used to destroy people. When you have the press pack after you, it is scary. When I did *Prayer for the Dying* with Mickey Rourke, Bob Hoskins and Alan Bates, that happened to me. Rourke played a member of the IRA. The film was re-edited without my approval and

I disowned it. The press, without ever seeing the film, decided I was an IRA supporter, the film was pro-IRA and because they [the producers] wanted to change it, I wanted to take my name off. I couldn't believe it. I was getting dangerously nasty mail. What I hadn't anticipated was the more you try to get out of a situation, the more interviews you give, the worse it becomes. When you are caught up in this journalistic feeding frenzy there is no way you are going to win. I got into a libel case with *The Mail on Sunday*. It meant two nerve-racking years. Me – I didn't have any money and I was taking on a powerful newspaper to clear my name. It was a re-run of *Sweet Smell of Success* and my own film, *Rumour*.

In a sense, I've always been going back to the theme explored in *Sweet Smell of Success*. It's informed everything I've done, not in terms of the way I've done it but in terms of the exploitation of people and the ruthless manner in which it is done. **"**

Thomas Vinterberg

Hearts of Darkness:
A Film-maker's Apocalypse

(Fax Bahr, George Hickenlooper,
1991)

The genial Dane Thomas Vinterberg was one of the 'little brothers' behind Dogme 95, the ten-point manifesto for low-budget film-making that shook up the independent film industry in the late 1990s. His second feature, *Festen*, was one of the sensations of the 1998 Cannes Film Festival. A brooding country-house drama that played like a twisted 90s version of Ingmar Bergman's *Smiles of a Summer Night* (1955), the film exposed the dysfunction and bitterness in a seemingly happy family whose members have come together to celebrate the father's sixtieth birthday. At this point, he seemed the golden boy of European cinema. However, there was a long hiatus between *Festen* and his next feature, the far bigger-budgeted English-language *It's All About Love* (2003). That film was received less kindly. Vinterberg then went on to make *Dear Wendy* (2005) from a script by his good friend Lars von Trier. An eccentric satire about guns and American teen culture that was set in the US but shot in Germany, this again received a mixed response.

Vinterberg was born in 1969 and grew up in a hippy commune in Copenhagen. In his work, perhaps railing against his family background, he has probed away at tension and dysfunction. His ability was evident from a very early stage. Vinterberg was only twenty years old when he enrolled at the National Film School of Denmark. His graduation short, *Last Round* (1993), was nominated for an Oscar. His first feature, *The Greatest Heroes* (1996), was acclaimed in Denmark, if not widely seen abroad. Then came *Festen*, which screened in Cannes alongside Lars von Trier's *The Idiots* and spearheaded an extraordinary flourishing of Danish cinema.

As a film-maker from a small country, Vinterberg was confronted by a familiar dilemma: whether to continue making modestly budgeted, local-language films or attempt to gatecrash the English-language market. Vinterberg's success with *Festen* began to seem double-edged. He risked being caught between two film-making traditions. At the time of writing (mid-2009), Vinterberg has completed one further Danish project, *A Man Comes Home*, and is in post-production on another, *Submarino*.

Thomas Vinterberg:

"What encouraged a radical change in my view of film-making, from just being something you do and a superficial matter of making intrigues on the screen, was the documentary *Hearts of Darkness*, about the making of *Apocalypse Now*. In a strange, lethal way, I was suddenly wildly attracted to the process of film-making, even though it is described as a nightmare – a matter of horror – in that film. There is a trance-like atmosphere. Suddenly, I was reminded that you can feel like it's a matter of life and death when you make a film. It changed from being a mediocre feeling of emptiness in your life to something that feels necessary. I realised that film-making can be many things – and it can be narcotic in a way. You can become addicted to it.

I saw *Hearts of Darkness* during my years at the Film School [in Copenhagen, 1989–93]. I watched it in my living room on some strange format from back then – maybe even U-Matic tape. I remember that the year after I had watched that film, I constantly related to it and referred to it. I remember the sentence said at the beginning, that this was not a film about war – it was war. When you're at film school, there is very big pressure on you. Maybe that is why I related to the film so much. I totally lived myself into the pressure that was on Francis Ford Coppola's shoulders. I completely understood the anxiety, all the expectations and the feeling of being a man completely alone in the middle of a huge organisation which you are entirely responsible for and which can go so utterly wrong. That is how we feel every time. The budget doesn't matter. In Coppola's case, it was a whole other scale. I am sure that didn't help him or make the pressure less. But it's a thing that all directors can relate to. Every morning when I wake up, I feel like, Jesus, how many years can I do this? When I saw *Hearts of Darkness*, I felt a sense of brotherhood with other directors. I realised this was how they all feel.

There is a weird sense of fulfilment [to film-making] that is narcotic. I don't think it is even the success a film might have. It's the whole sensation of being like a military organisation – there are one hundred people out there in the jungle. Even though you're in a Dogme film, that is how you feel. It is us against them. There is a lot of business around film-making, a lot of money and logistics – but people all have one common goal, which is to create a little bit of fragile life on the screen. A little bit of subtleness

Hearts of Darkness:
A Film-maker's
Apocalypse

and humanity. That combination feels very strong and very addictive – the combination of cold businesslike organisation and then, somewhere in the middle of that, being an artist and protecting the right to be a vulnerable person. It's somewhere in the mix of those two things that the feeling of a drug appears. I think maybe *Hearts of Darkness* gave me all the answers to feelings I already had. Also, of course, it gave me a horrifying perspective, in the sense that you are isolating yourself when you are making a film. It is not the real world. You are creating your own illusionary scenario. That's not even the film but the film behind the film – the crew, the shooting. That whole common psychosis that you're creating is not real life. It is time that you easily forget. When it is done, you can't even remember what happened. So it is dangerous. It is dangerous in the same way as drugs. You have a wonderful night and everyone is laughing in a common isolated room and then the next day, you can't remember it. It's not part of your life and not really part of your memory.

You know exactly where Coppola is. Normally, I find it ridiculous to watch other directors who consider what they do the most important thing in life. I find it humorous even, silly, but in this case, I found it frightening and respectful somehow. When I watched *Hearts of Darkness*, I knew what a masterpiece was coming out of it. It's a lesson too. It's important while you're making a film that you zoom out once in a while and objectively watch yourself and how far you are going – and yet do this without compromising your work. I had watched *Apocalypse Now* a couple of years before. I didn't know how chaotic the shooting had been. I didn't know all the stories about Harvey Keitel. So I was shocked [by the documentary], terribly shocked. It is one of those films where everything went wrong. I was in a trance-like condition after I had seen it and it encouraged me to go all the way. Maybe it [what Coppola was doing] was destructive, maybe it was delusional, but at least it was not mediocre, which is an even worse enemy. Having seen that film and having seen Coppola go all the way and be rewarded for it, that was encouraging. That was a feeling that must have been in the back of my head when we did Dogme, where I felt we jumped off the cliff and really did something that at that time was considered outrageous. Or with *It's All About Love* – that was a big, huge ship for us to put in the sea.

Fame was my attraction for wanting to become a film-maker. When I was fifteen or sixteen, I was a very, very shy boy and I had no self-esteem. I was very insecure. I thought that if I do something very good, then at least people will know who I am and then at least I have that advantage when I enter the room. I tried with my guitar but my friends were better. It bored me a little bit too. And being a rock star in Denmark is not big enough. When I started to make films, I felt very good about this whole communal thing. I grew up in a commune. This whole social aspect of being like a military organisation but being allowed to be preoccupied with things such as shyness or embarrassing love affairs, that whole combination I felt attracted to immediately. I also felt I had a talent for it. That I have been in doubt about many times since. I am in doubt every day but back then I had faith.

Film played no part whatsoever in the commune. They were all journalists, academics, philosophers and partiers. There were some musicians but they were mostly intellectual media people. If I hadn't applied to the film school, I probably would have ended up doing youth television.

To get into the film school, I had made a film about drugs called *Snowblind*, shot on U-matic high band. I entered the film school when I was nineteen. I got most of my basic knowledge about film when I was there. For me, it gave me everything as a film-maker. The five or six tricks I use now, I got them from there. I met good teachers and bad teachers. The whole basis of Dogme was invented at that school, the way of using limitations as your main inspiration was invented there because we had no money. We said let's make it an advantage we don't have any money. For me, it was highly uplifting even if it was personally one of the most brutal experiences I've had. They [the other students] are all my good friends, but it was highly competitive. When you learn a craft in theory, what you do becomes highly theoretical and doesn't work. The films that we did at film school (including those by Lars von Trier) were shit because they were so theoretical and so forced, so on a line and predictable. The teachers killed us for it. Many teachers are disillusioned film-makers themselves and they don't hold back. Every trace of self-confidence vanished. I did my graduate film in despair. I said, fuck it all, I'll make *Last Round*, a film about a man dying from cancer. I know you are sending me letters saying I am too young for this and therefore I can't do this, but I said this was the story I was going to do. It wasn't out of self-confidence. It was out of capitulation. Through that I found back my desire and playfulness. Maybe that's why my graduate film became the best film I have done.

You couldn't enter the Danish film school without being aware of Lars von Trier. He was breaking through on the European film scene with *Element of a Crime*. I saw that and was very impressed. But I saw what he did at film school, which was really shit up until this Tarkovsky seminar. Back then, he was very Tarkovsky-inspired.

It is very rare nowadays that I see films that I am very shaken by. I think Haneke has that quality now where I'm very fascinated. In my perspective, he is the most interesting film-maker in Europe right now. **"**

Albert Maysles

Captains Courageous

(Victor Fleming, 1937)

Albert Maysles is a legendary figure in the documentary world. Together with his brother and film-making partner David (who died in 1987), he was part of the 'direct cinema' movement of the early 1960s. This was the US answer to France's cinéma vérité – observational films often made with handheld equipment and avoiding authorial intrusion.

The Maysles tackled a wide range of subject matters. There was their funny and very poignant *Meet Marlon Brando* (1965), in which they filmed a number of hapless TV journalists interviewing the star. A bored and mischievous Brando parried and subverted their questions. Seen today, the short documentary plays like a premonitory satire about the inanities and excesses of celebrity journalism.

Salesman (1968) was the Maysles's documentary answer to Arthur Miller's *Death of a Salesman*, in which they followed four door-to-door bible salesmen from Boston on a selling trip to Florida. The film captures brilliantly that strange mix of ruthlessness and yearning that characterises the salesmen's lives: their aggression, which can border on cynicism, but also their belief in some kind of American dream that they still feel a part of, despite their tough experiences on the road. The brothers' other best-known films include *Gimme Shelter* (1970), which starts as a documentary about the Rolling Stones but ends as a chronicle of the shattering of the 1960s Utopian dream. The brothers record the Stones's concert at Altamont, which was brutally policed by Hell's Angels and at which one concertgoer was murdered.

By complete contrast, *Grey Gardens* (1976) was a study in American upper-class eccentricity – a portrait of a mother and her daughter (the aunt and cousin of Jackie Kennedy) living in decaying splendour in an East Hampton mansion that is running to seed.

Albert Maysles started off his career teaching psychology. His film-making began in the mid-1950s when he travelled to Russia, taking a 16mm camera with him to film the inmates of mental hospitals. In interviews, Maysles refers again and again to his background as a scientist and argues that it has always informed his choices as a film-maker. He aspires to a scientist's objectivity in his film work and always tries to keep 'point of view' at bay.

Albert Maysles:

"I am perhaps very unusual in that I had never seen many films. Most of what I put into my film-making hasn't come from other films but from experience as a psychologist and out of a need I felt originally to film people. First of all in the Soviet Union: *Psychiatry in Russia*. That was my first film way back in 1955. We had no direct visual understanding of ordinary life in Russia and so my motivation there was to put on film just who these people are. I am still motivated by trying to get close to people.

I don't think that the Italian realist film-makers had an influence on me but I see what they did as being very much parallel to my own work as a film-maker. Cesare Zavattini [the celebrated Italian neo-realist screenwriter] expressed it better than almost any documentary film-maker. He should have been a documentary film-maker. He pointed out how beneficial it would be to mankind to record on film what was going on in the real world. He meant it would be easier to love one another as we got to understand one another better. It's a two-way process. It goes back and forth. You understand and you love more. You love more and you understand more. I happened to meet him a few years ago and I was very much impressed with his philosophy, which matched my own.

I think of films like *Rocco and His Brothers* and *La strada*. But even when I saw *La strada*, almost every moment of it got me to think about an uncle of mine who sold eggs. He had a technique of selling them – he would crack the eggs and sold me eggs cheaper because they were cracked. That was his sort of deception. That was like the deception of Anthony Quinn. For all this deception, my uncle was somebody that very few people liked because he was so crude, and so forth. But we had a very good friendship. I would have loved to have made a film of him if he were alive when I had gotten into film-making. It could have been every bit as good as *La strada*.

I saw the neo-realist films as being make-believe films but having the flavour of reality that other films lacked. They seemed to be so real. It wasn't that there were famous actors or any of the Hollywood glamour there.

I remember seeing a film called *Captains Courageous*, which was a famous film of its time. As with other films, I got so excited that when the film was over, I just ran like hell. It was the same kind of excitement that Tolstoy felt when he saw his first film in 1910. He decided that there was no more point in writing because the motion picture captures it all so truthfully. I saw it in a cinema in Boston. I just remember that one. But there is nothing specific

Captains Courageous

SCREEN EPIPHANIES

from that film that carries over into my own film-making.

My most important influence was being a social scientist and a psychologist. It made my work as a documentary film-maker all the more objective. I didn't favour a point of view which I was trying to prove. Rather, I went into it with a totally open mind, which one does hopefully as a scientist. I was disposed to making documentaries in a fashion completely the opposite of, let's say, Michael Moore. My mother taught me something that was a very important part of my upbringing, which was that there was good in everybody. Once again, I never used my film-making to make somebody look good and bad. Rather, the idea was to go into it with a sense of discovery.

I had done some still photography. When I was a kid, maybe ten years old, I picked up a camera and started taking pictures and developing film. It was an art I took to immediately. A natural way of expressing myself artistically. I had bought a camera for 35 cents from a hardware store. I don't know why. Nobody told me. I had no idea how I got interested. I could see that I was good enough at it that I could really go into it professionally. But then I thought that just taking still photographs was not enough. I wanted to do something with greater impact and once I started

making documentary movies, I could see that that was my perfect profession.

People told me my still photography was pretty much like that of Henri Cartier-Bresson, who was a photographer without prejudice. Maybe five years after I had begun my film-making, I met Bruce Davidson. Is that a name familiar to you? He was a famous American Magnum photographer who also introduced me to Cartier-Bresson.

I had never seen any of the films by Ricky Leacock or D. A. Pennebaker. I got to know them by working with them. Ricky spoke a great deal of his experience with Robert Flaherty. At some point – I don't know where or when – I did see *Nanook of the North*. I was so well along with the advancements we were making with the new equipment and philosophy that I was impressed with Flaherty only in that I could see that, given the tools he had at the time, he was able to do wonderful work. But we had pushed the medium far beyond that.

I am making a film now about people who meet on trains. It is really a collection of short stories. *Rocco and His Brothers* begins at the railway station, as the family move up from the south to seek a new life in the north. If that was real, it could have been a sequence in my films.

Celebrity has been a bit of a diversion from my basic interest in ordinary people. *Salesman* is more akin to what I want to do if I have the opportunity to do something on my own instigation. The other films, I believe in the films – they are wonderful films – but the opportunity to do them and the money to make them came in odd ways. Granada Television called me up one day and said that the Beatles were arriving in two hours – did I want to make a film of them? And they paid for it. *Gimme Shelter* – a friend of mine told me that the Stones were in town: maybe there is a film there and so I went ahead and met them. And I went ahead and made that film. With Muhammad Ali, someone came to me directly connected with Ali – and so I had the money and the entry for that film. I have made a lot of films about celebrities simply because they were projects that came to me.

Salesman gave me full proof that if you wait it out, things will happen. Of course, we started with the hypothesis that there would be drama. So many times when the salesmen knocked on the door, we got into a whole new situation of selling. There was that already – the major possibility. The world is rich with scenes, events, things going on that are fruit for our endeavours and it helps to have a knack for putting ourselves at the right place at the right time. I think I have that knack. And I have quite a talent for getting access to people

where others might not succeed. I not only get access to people. As I am filming, I have no difficulty in maintaining a rapport where I have full acceptance. I feel quite confident I can take on the responsibility of telling the truth about another person's life. And then that attention must be paid. I am paying that attention. I am therefore doing something of good for the film, for the people I film, for the people who have the opportunity to share the experience of the process that I am filming. And I like people. And I trust people. All of that generates a rapport of mutual trust.

Being my own subject? I haven't really gotten deeply into that film yet. I think that I can do as decent a job making a film about myself. Nobody's film is that person alone. I work with other people and so there will be at least a couple of more people working with me. The responsibility will be shared.

That is a tendency that many film-makers have – that they have got to fulfil a point of view. That point of view might not be sustainable in actual fact if one approached the subject with an open mind. Having this point of view limits one's perspective. People like Fred Wiseman, especially in his earlier films, had this good guy, bad guy approach. In fact, with Wiseman's *Titicut Follies*, I have learned that in the mental hospital that comes under such severe attack in his film, the administrators were already well along in improving things. None of that is given recognition by the film-maker. On the other hand, he is not even serving the patients very well by simply using them as mannequins and filming them at their most psychotic state. He was actually not making his point because he was dehumanising the patients.

We are only human. We all have our frame of reference. I heard a lecture on Shakespeare. The last part of the lecture was to the effect that Shakespeare's greatness lay in part in the fact that he could distance himself from a point of view. That is probably the best way to put out. I feel as strongly as ever that one should approach things with an open mind. I enjoy that kind of serendipitous adventure. Maybe that is one of the reasons I have chosen this profession. I haven't lost that kind of strictness. It comes from my scientific training and a love of humanity, if you will. They say that love is blind. I see love as being blind to prejudice. Love is open to discovery and appreciation of humanity – we sure as hell need it in this country. The mass media seem to be devoted to dehumanising [people] in every way possible. The television commercial is almost a perfect example of dehumanisation – wonderful photography without a heart or soul. In the movies, we see automobiles exploding and violence of one sort of another. When my daughter was four, many years ago, I took her to pick up the *New York Times*. We got to the news-stand and the paper hadn't arrived yet. She turned to me and said, 'Daddy, the paper is not ready. The people haven't been killed yet.'

In 1954, I travelled all over Western Europe on a motorcycle. I guess I am an adventurer basically. I love to go to new places and discover things. I realised that in 1955 the Soviet Union was the one place we needed to know so much more about and we were getting very little direct information, especially the familiarity with ordinary people. That is what motivated me. When I arrived in the Soviet Union, I met a reporter who tried to get an invitation for me to attend a reception at the Romanian Embassy. He wasn't able to but I went there anyway, I crashed the party and I met the top, top, top Soviet leaders. They were as curious about me as I was about them. One of them gave me the commission to film in the mental hospitals. That is how that happened. Once I got into that film, I could see I was in a league beyond still photography. Just this year, I looked back at the photographs I took many years ago.

Epiphanies? I have probably seen fewer films than most people. **99**

Sally Potter

Monsieur Hulot's Holiday

(Jacques Tati, 1953)

Sally Potter, a petite English-born writer-director-dancer, was born in 1949. She went to 'a horrid, Victorian school full of cruel people' in Wiltshire, and was briefly a pupil at Gospel Oak Primary School in London, which wasn't much of an improvement. Potter was hardly a conventional 'middle-class, middlebrow' English kid. 'My father was an anarchist,' she declares. 'Not a bomb-throwing one, but somebody who believed in freedom of the individual and not bowing down to the authorities. I grew up in an anarchist family who were atheist, who loved music, and who didn't have much money. Our fortunes were erratic. I know what it is to be poor, let's put it that way.'

Norman Potter (who died in 1995) was a carpenter, poet and designer. His career encompassed both stints as a tutor at the Royal College of Art and several months behind bars at Wandsworth prison and Wormwood Scrubs, where he'd been sent in the early 1940s – or so one of his obituaries proclaimed – 'after an unsuccessful attempt to initiate a moral debate on the nature of war with a military tribunal'. Potter's mother was a singer who had a brief career on the stage and taught music to children. Both her grandmothers were actresses. 'I was very close to my maternal grandmother, who was half French and who in the 1920s was indeed in cabaret and did a mixture of singing and dancing. I'm sure that some of my attraction to the world of showbusiness and opera was more or less in my blood.'

Given such a background and her own early experiences as a film-maker, it's not hard to see why Potter might be bitter about England. Her first feature, the BFI-backed *The Gold Diggers* (1983), starring Julie Christie and made by an all-woman crew, disappeared without trace in the UK. *Orlando* (1992) and *The Tango Lesson* (1997) were international co-productions that would never have been made if she had had to rely on English backing alone.

Like Peter Greenaway, Potter seems more appreciated on the Continent than at home. Nevertheless, she refuses to accept old stereotypes about stolid, philistine little England. 'Beneath every English stiff upper lip, there lurks a trembling, passionate one,' she suggests. Scrape away the phoney patriotism, the sense of Empire, 'and all the other oppressive aspects of Englishness', and she finds much to cherish: 'the self-mocking humour, the respect for individual liberty, the love of gardening, the not to be underestimated power of the rose', she muses, sounding a little like George Orwell in *The Lion and the Unicorn*. And, no, the English aren't that bad at dancing either. They're not a patch on the Argentinians she worked with on *The Tango Lesson*, but 'we're getting better, [we've got] some really good jivers, some great ballet dancers, and just look at Scottish [sic] country dancing ... the English are quite good movers and shakers'.

Potter is accustomed to making films in improvised and hurried circumstances. This dates back from her days shooting experimental films at the London Film-makers' Co-op. 'There's never enough time, there's never enough money … it's just a change of scale,' she says of the difference between making 8mm shorts and shooting a Hollywood epic like her feature *The Man Who Cried* (2000).

There is a sense now that her career is coming full circle. Her latest film, *Rage*, which premiered at the 2009 Berlin Festival, was shot in double-quick time. Set against the backcloth of the New York fashion industry, the film features an all-star cast (including Jude Law and Judi Dench). However, Potter only had two days with each cast member. 'It's a very no-waste production. I saw it as a celebration of "poor" cinema,' Potter explains, 'something that goes back absolutely to the elements of storytelling on film.'

The film-maker bridles at the suggestion that some of her earlier work (for instance, *I Am an Ox, I Am a Horse, I Am a Man, I Am a Woman*, her 1988 film on women in Soviet Cinema) was on the esoteric side. 'Even when I made my tiny little 8mm films, I always dreamed of them being in the Odeon, Leicester Square, and I couldn't understand why nobody else agreed with me at the time.'

Sally Potter:

"I like the word 'epiphany'. It's better than a 'top 10' or a 'top 1' or any other such impossibility. The nature of the history of cinema is that there is this plethora and the points of reference are multiple and they all interrelate. As Michael Powell said, all is one. You feel as if you are looking at different parts of a prism. To isolate one particular film is a kind of non-starter. But I think the feeling of epiphany, which is an almost transcendent or inspirational moment when the light comes in, makes sense for me at different moments with different films. It is cumulative. Thinking of you, I tried to find one from a list but in fact, as I started to write the list, I thought of another, and then I remembered another, and so it became a kind of associative chain of reference, which seems to me like the cinemagoing experience – one film leads to another.

My childhood viewing was rather restricted by my mother, who was otherwise an extremely liberal person with almost no controls on my life, but she really didn't want me or my brother to watch anything violent or disturbing when we were children. So we saw certain films over and over and over again, notably *Monsieur Hulot's Holiday*, *Singin'*

in the Rain, *Seven Brides for Seven Brothers* and all the Marx brothers. Those – and some of the Ealing comedies – that combination of viewing had a real impact on me.

My father was an anarchist – a self-defined one. He was anti-authoritarian, libertarian – he had the idea that people should be able to make decisions about their own life and not be in the service of the State. He believed that it's when people are obedient en masse that we have wars and murder. If people respect independent thought and joined together, [he felt] we wouldn't have that. My mother wouldn't have called herself an anarchist but would have thought of herself as having a liberal outlook and a way of seeing the world that was quite heavily conditioned by the arts. They weren't particularly interested in cinema. My father was a designer more interested in poetry and furniture (the modern movement, the Bauhaus and so on) than in cinema. He had a good soft spot for Bergman. My mother's passion was music. She had wanted to be a singer. But she loved those films she took us to.

As a child, I probably knew every frame of *Monsieur Hulot's Holiday*. I knew the sequences off by heart. I think what indelibly struck me was not so much

Monsieur Hulot's
Holiday

the comedy of it, which often felt slow, as the compassion in the observation: this observation of small moments, a swinging door. The emptiness of the soundtrack, which just has one or two effects dropped into it. Almost the feeling of it as a kind of meditation on loneliness and the social behaviour of people attempting to have a good time. It was the tragic part of the comedy that impressed me and the minimalism of the means with which it was realised. I think as a child I was experiencing it as a minimalist transcendent meditation more than as the work of a comic genius. I just quickly looked up something about Tati before you came and discovered something which I hadn't known before, which was that he lived most of his life in poverty, having to raise mortgages on his previous films to raise money for the next ones. The solitariness of that position as a film-maker I realised was imbuing the films themselves with the melancholy. I found that a fascinating piece of hidden information about the work.

I had a similar feeling with the Marx brothers – a feeling that they were philosophers and that this was a worldview that was being [shown on screen]. It was an irreverent worldview. *Duck Soup* is the best anti-war film ever made,

with everything done so subtly, so much at a tangent and so much with wit, and so much with exploding the form they were in. Their films felt like an endless box of jewels. Again, there was compassion and the ironic observation of idiocy. There was a sequence I always loved in *A Night at the Opera* with the parody of the first part, the parody of the second part – all that contractual, bureaucratic garbage stuff.

Subsequently, I found the Marx brothers and *Monsieur Hulot's Holiday* stagy and slow in a way that I didn't when I first saw them – very fourth wall-oriented, not thoroughly cinematic. But I still find them matchless in their irreverence, inventiveness and general all-round anarchism.

Singin' in the Rain was probably my first introduction to a study of the nature of cinema itself. It's a kind of love affair/deconstruction of the joys and nonsenses, artifices and comedies of the history of the form itself. There was a complete acceptance of the artificiality of the form – a surrender to the joy of the fiction. I always thought of musicals as not so much light entertainment, although there was huge joy in them, but as an irreverent explosion of the form, with non-literal narrative and all of that. All of those people, Tati,

Duck Soup (Leo McCarey, 1933)

the Marx brothers and the actors in *Singin' in the Rain*, were all very physical performers. Their films involved dance and music to some degree. Groucho was very verbal, but with a walk! They weren't naturalistic or ordinary.

The sequence of the actual 'Singing in the Rain', I remembered as a child writing to *Children's Favourites* on the radio to request that they played it. They did, with Uncle Muck saying make sure you put on your wellington boots when you go out.

Bicycle Thieves was very different from the Marx brothers and Jacques Tati, but I remember the portrait of the father and son and of poverty – the sense that a film could open out that untold story and make it visible with such beauty and such love. Seeing that was an absolutely crucial part of my development as a film-maker. *L'Atalante* likewise had a tenderness for the characters and love for the medium.

In my fairly early teens, sixteen or seventeen, having been a devourer of Russian literature and read all those Dostoesvky books, I discovered Eisenstein, Pudovkin and Vertov and the others through a film society. I lived in Bethnal Green and there was a film society attached to the art college. I was blown away not just by the montage

(which even then felt a bit heavy-handed to me) but by the way you could feel the life project behind the film. This wasn't just about making a film about interesting events. It was about changing the world. There was equally value placed on exploding the form and developing a new language as there was on changing the society. It was the artist as revolutionary. Not the message in it, but the dedication and thrill of the form, the ride we were taken on with the form, before Stalin closed it down. That was the beginning of my total immersion in cinema. It was every day and every night – not just the film society but everything I could lay my hands on anywhere. I was watching all of the French New Wave, all of the early Russians, some early Indian cinema, Satyajit Ray, Bergman, Kurosawa and the real avant-gardists – Warhol's *Empire State*, Michael Snow's *Wavelength*. The one-take films that I found completely fascinating.

I had made my first film at fourteen. It was an 8mm film. I had announced that I was going to be a film-maker. I was lent an 8mm camera by my uncle, who was in a relationship with an underground American film-maker. They encouraged me in my youthful ambitions but they were the only ones

POTTER / *Monsieur Hulot's Holiday*

who did. My parents were encouraging but were very busy with their own lives and preoccupations. They said, oh, fine. It wasn't like being pushed, encouraged or indeed trained. I have no training. But the desire was there. I had already seen *Last Year in Marienbad* and I must have seen *The Third Man*, which was hugely influential, not least because of its relationship with music. I had also probably seen quite a lot of Powell and Pressburger. I left school so early (at sixteen) and then home immediately as well. I wanted to be a film director and as far as I was concerned, I wasn't learning anything at school. In fact, school seemed to be about holding me back and stopping me from doing almost everything I wanted to do in life. There was no undergraduate training for film at that point in the way there is now. There was the Royal College of Art postgraduate. I went to them and asked if they would consider taking me. They pretty much laughed in my face. They said everyone wants to be in the movies, dear. I had an 8mm film to show.

At the time, there was no word like 'independent' film. There was 'underground' film but really there were the movies – the big films you saw at the pictures. I don't think I would have known what a runner was, for example.

I just started with what I could, which was to pick up a camera and make something. My 8mm film didn't have a name. It was a little visual poem with all the editing in the camera. I took a friend and shot in the street. It was in black and white. It might be the shape of a wheel or a wall. It was compositional and visual primarily. I would have thought of it as having a visual rhythm and might even have called it a poem. I am sure that even then, in my mind, it related to those big films, but I couldn't figure out how to get from A to B: from where I was to where they were. But my decision to leave school was entirely around the fantasy that I would just launch myself out into space and somehow become a film-maker. It was and is precarious [laughs]. I knew that how I was going to learn about film-making was through watching those films.

At the beginning, I was a bit alone. Later, I joined the London Film-makers' Co-operative – and then I was even more alone! I didn't really share many of the structuralist-dominated ideas of the time. But I did love this fact that there was building with a room in it and an old editing bench on it and a dusty old camera – and I could go in there and figure out how to use it. I really had my hands in the chemicals, my hands on the Steenbeck, and I learned by watching and by doing. I think I was self-guided to some extent. If I saw one Bergman, I would have wanted to see more. I would have read something in the paper about Godard and found it exciting, followed that, and it would have led to something else – and so on.

The Powell and Pressburger films were very important for me. I remember *The Red Shoes* as a child and also seeing *A Matter of Life and Death*. I was very aware of their oeuvre and only later came to understand some of the alchemy that made it up – the Britishness of Michael Powell, the European Jewishness of Pressburger and the entrepreneurial genius of Alexander Korda. That led to some incredibly interesting things. *The Saragossa Manuscript* had a very big influence on me because of its cyclical structure where you keep entering into a new story. It's labyrinthine, with a Borges feeling to it. It influenced me a lot from a structural point of view.

Many of the films that are made now are coming from a place and a motivation that I experience as limited: they're somehow calculated and without that sense of emotional, spiritual and political openness and risk-taking. People play safe because it's so difficult to finance films. That glorious feeling of adventure you don't come across that often. Channel 4 and the BBC have turned down everything I've ever proposed in my entire life's work. I have a record of zero with them. All of the public bodies have always turned down most of what I've proposed. Most of the funding of my films has come from outside the UK. I'm the only director I know who's turned down every offer to direct a commercial. **”**

Nick Park

Rebecca

(Alfred Hitchcock, 1940)

With four Academy Awards to his credit already, animator Nick Park has a fair claim as the most successful British director of his generation. He created Wallace and Gromit, claymation, plasticine figures who've become household names internationally. With his pullover, big ears and thick Lancashire accent, Wallace is a very British figure: a bluff, eccentric inventor. Gromit, meanwhile, is a lovable beagle with a melancholic but very expressive face.

Park is part of Aardman Animations in Bristol, having joined the company in the mid-1980s. One quality that makes him (and the company he works for) fascinating is the way he maintains a local identity despite the huge international success that has come Aardman's way. There is a modesty and self-deprecating humour about him that you don't always find in multiple Oscar winners. Aardman has worked with some very big Hollywood studios, first with Dreamworks and now with Sony. Nonetheless, the company has kept its Bristol base, while Park has continued working in the same spirit that characterised his early films, *A Grand Day Out* and *Creature Comforts* (both 1989).

In *A Matter of Loaf and Death*, the Wallace and Gromit adventure premiered on British TV at Christmas 2008, the deadpan humour remained resolutely British. The title self-consciously invoked the memory of Powell and Pressburger's *A Matter of Life and Death* (1946), a classic of British 1940s cinema. Park is steeped in British film-making of that era. Like many Brits of his generation, he also acknowledges the strong formative influence of Oliver Postgate (the creator of *Noggin the Nog* and *The Clangers*) as well as his admiration for Tony Hart, the animator behind kids' TV series *Vision On*.

Nick Park:

" I've actually been wondering what to choose as my epiphany. My problem is that I can't pin down anything really. There is one film that comes to mind that I've probably enjoyed more than any other, just in terms of what I get from it, and that is Hitchcock's *Rebecca*. I can watch that and keep on going back to it – savouring the drama, the photography and the story. I saw it when I was at college at Sheffield Polytechnic back in the late 70s. I think I saw it in the holidays, as an afternoon matinee, on the TV. I love Sunday matinees. It evokes all of that, really. I love just sitting down and watching an old black-and-white film. I was studying model animation – all sorts of animation, really, on a communication arts course which comprised film and photography. It was a crash course in film-making. We had film studies and watched all sorts of films from the history of film-making. I would draw my inspiration from all these things, really, as well as animation.

With *Rebecca*, first of all it's a Daphne Du Maurier novel. He [Hitchcock] is standing on her shoulders really. It is the way he brought it to the screen. He is such a visual film-maker. It's the way

he dealt with the Mrs Danvers character, the evil housekeeper who is keeping the old Mrs De Winter's memory alive. It's the intrigue, the story – I just love mystery and intrigue and the way Hitchcock deals with it as well – the way the whole story is about somebody who is dead. Film-making is a meeting of many skills: photography, acting, execution, costume, music – the whole choreography. I love the way she [Mrs Danvers] is portrayed in a very simple and well-defined way – not just dialogue but visually as well. It's the way Hitchcock gets her to float around, as if she has no legs. She is very ghostlike. She very much haunts the place. There is a particular scene I have always relished when she is trying to drive the new Mrs De Winter [Joan Fontaine] insane and to kill herself – she is talking about Rebecca as if she still exists, as if she is still there. She does believe it as well, I think. She is mad in a beautifully executed way, mad in an interesting way – you love her as a character as well. You so sympathise with the Joan Fontaine character, with the situation she is in and the world she has entered, with her distant husband, who is obviously saddened and distracted. There is a massive kind of reversal. You think he still loves Rebecca and then you find out he never did. I love all of that, just the art of the film-making – the way you can withhold information.

Animation suggests movement all the time. For me, it is very much about knowing when not to move things and how to dramatise. I see slightly the influence of Mrs Danvers coming through in the penguin in *The Wrong Trousers*. It's nowhere near the same level but the way Steve Box, my fellow animator on that film, dealt with the character and the way we talked about it was as if the penguin was a Mrs Danvers – very kept, very constrained in movement, and so movement becomes more meaningful. We could easily have portrayed a penguin with a funny waddle or something – the way you would expect animation to do it.

I just found *Rebecca* very absorbing on many levels, particularly story. You are immediately drawn in. Even the first line – 'last night, I dreamed I went to Manderley again' – I just love that beginning, the way you are drawn in.

There is a whole lot of films of that ilk. The Ealing comedies were heavily influential on me, films like *The Ladykillers* that were always on TV. I tend just to pick things up, take them in and store them up somewhere. I do love to sit and just observe. It's hard to say why

something works for you. I like the oddness of the characters in the Ealing films.

When I was growing up, *The Clangers* and all that work by Oliver Postgate and Peter Firmin were a big influence. There was a certain quirkiness to it. It is easy to underestimate the appeal that has to kids – the fact that it was slightly out of the ordinary. As a kid, you don't know that it is out of the ordinary. It is strange and inviting – and you gravitate to that – the strange world that they created. There is an atmosphere. I used to love it when those came on TV. It's funny but I wasn't so into *Bagpuss*. (Now I appreciate it.) Even though we only had three channels [of TV], there was amazing variety and odd things in the mix of the general daily diet of what you saw. There was a strange diversity and imagination [to the programming]. I remember the films that used to be played on BBC2. I loved being drawn in, whether by comic books or TV drama. Now it seems a lot more designed for audiences and audience figures. I remember films like *The Red Ballon*, which I saw after school. That would come on BBC2.

I used to wonder how they got cars to go off cliffs in *The Saint* or whatever. I used to think there must be people who don't mind dying who would queue

Rebecca

up for that job. I remember my dad explaining to me how animation is done. You'd see something on *Blue Peter* or on a programme like *Tom Tom*. I started making films when I was about twelve years old. I think being an artist and cartoonist, I realised how it was done. But it was the magic of it that drew me in. I loved the way that I could create an illusion. My father was a photographer by trade, mainly of architecture. I loved his cameras – looking at them and knowing how they worked.

One of the earliest really big influences on me was Ray Harryhausen. I was young, ten or eleven, and absolutely obsessed with dinosaurs. This was long before everybody was interested in them, really. I didn't know anyone else who was, actually. I knew all the names. I used to have models of dinosaurs and I used to think how much I would love to make films with them in, like Ray Harryhausen. *One Million Years BC* was one of my favourites. I used to think how much I would love to make films that put people in with dinosaurs. *King Kong*, the 1933 *King Kong*, was a big epiphany for me, actually, because I couldn't believe what I was seeing. I remember seeing the clips advertising it. I couldn't wait to see it. I couldn't believe that such a thing existed. And

then Ray Harryhausen's work took over. I set about making my own dinosaurs and planning to animate them. I made them out of foam rubber and coat-hangers. For the skin, I was going to use some old nylon tights and spray-paint it. I never actually filmed that dinosaur. What took over was drawing cartoons and animating them, and making models of them.

Of course, I was taken off to see the Disney films. The first one I saw was *Snow White*. I was about six years old. I was absolutely terrified by the witch – by the old stepmother. But I loved it. I loved being terrified. That was a very strong memory. Other Disney films like *Alice in Wonderland* – I loved being in there, absorbed in that world. I always remember the shock of coming out. You know, the red buses and ordinary life on drizzly streets. I remember that big jolt. I was so absorbed. It was a very big jolt back into reality. That was more traumatic than the horror of the film, really.

Preston had three cinemas on the main high street – an ABC, an Odeon and another one, I think. I would go fairly regularly. I used to go to ABC minors on a Saturday morning and see the double feature. One of the first films was *The Man from U.N.C.L.E.* I used to go with my dad because he liked spy stories. He liked James Bond. I saw *You Only Live Twice*. That was one of my first films as well. I would go with my dad sometimes in the evening and with my brother. I loved the experience of going to the cinema. It was quite a magical experience. I would see a variety of films. I had seen Ray Harryhausen on *Screen Test* [a TV show about cinema for kids]. A friend and I were quite excited about the next Harryhausen film coming out and would go and see it.

I always saw my film-making just as a hobby, really. I was a strange child in that I never thought anyone would be interested in what I was doing. I just thought – I am interested in that and I love the idea of doing it. I sort of didn't take myself seriously. It was because it was cartoons. I liked drawing cartoons and just making people laugh with plasticine men falling over or having their heads accidentally cut off or something. I just thought it was fun and that it wasn't art.

Later, when I did a foundation art course, I didn't even tell the tutors that I did animation. I had done about half a dozen films at home but I didn't think they [the tutors] would think that it was serious. It was only my private hobby which my family would enjoy. When the tutors did see it [the animation], they were incredulous that I hadn't mentioned it. My mum and my dad always were very encouraging, actually. If we had a skill, they wanted us to use it. They encouraged all of us to do arts. There were five kids in the family. I was the middle one. They would help provide paper for us to draw with all the time. It was usually scraps and stuff from work. They were always encouraging. When I showed an interest to use the holiday movie camera, they were more than encouraging.

I remember initially when we first got our cine-camera – a Bell and Howell 8mm camera – they said we should think up some ideas and go and make some films. I was the only one that took that up, really. I was really into drawing cartoons. I thought that one day I might be a cartoon artist for *The Beano* or something like that. That was too ambitious, really. In a way, there was a film-making aspect, almost like storyboarding. I got books out from the library and saw that Hitchcock often used (in *Psycho*, for example) storyboards. I started drawing my own storyboards, thinking in a filmic kind of way.

I did a BA Fine Arts in Communication Arts. By then, I had got the idea that I could do film-making. I did A levels and Foundation at the same time in Preston.

While I was there, I remember it suddenly dawning on me when my tutors found out that I did animation at home. They said, why didn't you tell us? You could be doing that here, on a course. We would love you to do that. I was dealing with fun. I was dealing with cartoons and slapstick. Then, my dad said maybe I could think of doing a degree course in film-making. That was beyond anything I had ever imagined. I thought that was only for other people who lived in the south – or people who had lived near film studios and Hollywood. Suddenly, this world became somewhere I could go. I don't know whether it was just on my own behalf, whether I felt there was this [snobbery]. In a way, it has always been a problem taking myself seriously as a legitimate kind of film-maker and storyteller. I always wanted to be taken seriously as a film-maker more than just an animator. The fact that I have been able to do animation and impress people by making things move in a funny way or whatever or with humour, that has been my ticket into the film industry. I might not have made it otherwise.

After Sheffield, I went to film school [the National Film School]. I thought Colin Young [the school's principal] was Orson Welles! I just thought wow! These are real film industry people – they seem to all know what they are talking about. I was just totally impressed by the world. It was getting nearer to London. Beaconsfield was in that green belt where all the studios are. I was just on a high, really. It was quite a shock, actually, that all these people I thought were so sophisticated and talked so intellectually about films and theory suddenly, when they saw my work, just had a big belly laugh. It was like a dawning on me. I suddenly realised that it was not that difficult. I suddenly found that as much as they would all talk about film theory in all these different workshops, everybody liked to see something that was just funny. There has been a part of me that thinks I should be doing something more serious all the time. There is a serious side, actually, that wants to make films. I have always felt the need to tell stories that have some type of integrity in themselves, that isn't just pure comedy. I have always been looking for some kind of depth. That is what it is really about. Often, my ideas aren't funny – the ambitions of the things I want to do, but the comedy is what keeps me going. It is the satisfaction of making the jokes work. But it is also about making the story work and the drama work.

The challenge is to hold on to the innocence. I don't think we've been immersed in the commercial side.

Where did Wallace and Gromit come from? It was a coming together of a number of things for me. I was searching for ages during my first year at film school what to do for my graduation project. I had done model animation, very influenced by 3D *Noggin the Nog*. It was because of what clay and plasticine animation gives you – you've got the flexibility of the drawn cartoon and there is the 3D-ness of it. You can light it and use the camera in a live-action manner. It was a coming together of a love of all these Ealing films, Hitchcock films and Tex Avery cartoons. I remember one moment of epiphany when I was trying to decide what to do. I was heavily into plasticine animation. I was at the Annecy animation festival and saw a whole programme of Pluto cartoons. Suddenly, it occurred to me that I had never seen this kind of animation done with plasticine. Model animation tends to be rather staid and rather stagy and slow. I thought, well, I love story, adventure and mystery – why not combine all these things and put it into an animated film?

I sometimes sit down and watch an old Norman Wisdom film. I find that quite inspiring. I grew up with that. It was always a treat when Norman Wisdom came on the telly. **”**

Sir Alan Parker

Little Fugitive

(Ray Ashley, Morris Engel,
Ruth Orkin, 1953)

Alan Parker
filming *Midnight
Express* (1978)

Alan Parker is a belligerent and combative figure: a working-class director from Islington, north London, who will never step away from a fight. He is one of a number of British directors (among the others were Hugh Hudson, Adrian Lyne and Ridley Scott) who emerged in the 1970s from the advertising industry. What distinguished him from many of his fellow Brits was that he wrote his own screenplays and was able to work successfully in Hollywood without compromising or becoming a director-for-hire. His films invariably made money, and he was always involved in every aspect of them, from screenplay to editing to marketing.

His relationship with the British film industry establishment is ambivalent. A skilled cartoonist and satirist, he didn't conceal his contempt for public-funded arthouse film-making. Parker referred witheringly to Peter Greenaway's *The Draughtsman's Contract* (1982) as 'The Draughtsman's Con Trick'. In the mid-1980s, he made an acerbic documentary called *A Turnip's Head Guide to British Cinema*. However, at the beginning of the Tony Blair era, in 1997, he accepted a position as Chairman of the British Film Institute. Later, he became the first Chairman of the UK Film Council, the national cinema agency set up during the early Blair era. There was a sense that he was moving toward the establishment. However, in his public pronouncements, he remained as outspoken as ever. In one highly contentious 2002 speech, 'Building a Sustainable UK Film Industry', he berated the 'Little England' and 'cultural Canute' mentality of film-makers and policymakers who didn't share his vision of film as an international industry. Parker advocated that the Brits partner with the US to ensure their movies were distributed globally. This was not a message that many in the UK industry wanted to hear. Parker, it was clear, relished jolting them out of their complacency.

Parker believes that his advertising background explains the dismissive, high-handed way in which he has sometimes been treated by British critics. 'I started that way because there was very little else one could do at the time.' He left school at eighteen. With his background and qualifications, he says, it would not have been possible to get a job as a trainee director at the BBC. 'And there were no media studies courses or anything like that. So I went into advertising as a copywriter instead.'

Parker began writing and shooting commercials with a 16mm camera he found in his ad agency basement. Shooting commercials for everything from spirits to frozen dinners, he ended up making miniature, 30-second versions of 'every movie I've ever loved, everything from *Oliver Twist* to *Brief Encounter*. It was our film school. It allowed us to film continuously every single week.'

Right from their earliest days in advertising, he and his colleagues David Puttnam and Charles Saatchi dreamed of breaking into the film business. Both he and Saatchi wrote their first screenplays around the same time. 'Mine ended up getting made – Charles's didn't. So he said, fuck this, I'm going to go into advertising big-time. It could have been the other way round. If his script had been made and mine hadn't, I might have ended up the owner of the biggest advertising agency in the world with the finest collection of modern art.'

Parker has always been one of the most visceral of directors. Sweat and spectacle are the two common ingredients in nearly all his films. Even he admits he sometimes goes a little over the top. When he was filming the climactic scene in *Midnight Express*, in which the young American prisoner (Brad Davis) bites out the Turkish prison warder's tongue, he remembers, he 'got a bit carried away'. He and his camera operator forced the unfortunate Davis to spit out a pig's tongue over and over again while they tried to capture the character's sense of bloody exhilaration. 'We were shooting in the *kogus* – the central area of the prison. We must have been doing the scene for 15 minutes. I turned around at the end and there was no crew. They were all so disgusted with what I was doing that they had gone out. There were sixty people in the yard behind, waiting for me to finish the scene.'

Parker cites *The Commitments* (1991), his rollicking tale about a young Dublin soul band, as the most enjoyable film he has ever worked on. What he relished most was the sheer camaraderie.

When he is not working, he gets very itchy feet. 'It's that feeling you get when you arrive on set at some ridiculous hour,' he rhapsodises, 'it is just getting light and you're having a sausage roll as the camera is rolled out on a dolly.' Even today, Parker says, he is still driven by the same enthusiasm about film that first fired him when he was a kid. 'Growing up in Islington, I went to the cinema as often as I could – the Carlton, Essex Road, the Blue Hall or the Odeon, Upper Street (that used to be a penny more). How I used to love it …'

Alan Parker:

"Is it ever one film or one moment and at what point in your life? I've tried to go back to the original time when I thought film was more than going to the local Odeon. I grew up in Islington when Saturday-morning pictures was our introduction to seeing films. It was kids of all ages and it was unbelievably noisy. It was bedlam. Everybody talked. There were fights going on and goodness knows what. As I grew older, when I was about fourteen, I became a monitor. You had to keep the kids quiet, little kids who were running all over the place. It was absolute madness. In the programme, you would see ten different things: anything they could get their hands on basically. Any old scratchy film that was available and was suitable for children would be chucked up there. You would see rubbish and then, every so often, you would see something wonderful. I was the oldest kid, but then, when I was fourteen, I got into the football team at school and I had to stop going. It was a great tragedy for me that I had to play football instead of going to Saturday-morning pictures.

I don't know if I had many epiphanies there but I do remember a film when I was very young, and then there are films that have influenced me as I have got older.

When I was very young, most of my filmgoing was to the local Odeon for Saturday-morning pictures. It sounds pretty ridiculous now, when there are so many ways in which you can see films. I came from a background where I wouldn't dream of going to the National Film Theatre and so I didn't really know about that stuff. All I knew about or could absorb was what was playing locally in my little world, in a triangle between the Odeon on Upper Street, a cinema on Essex Road and a couple of cinemas at the Angel. I very rarely went with my parents. They went to see their things. The films changed twice a week. My mother was quite an avid filmgoer. I went with her sometimes, but very rarely. I was about ten or eleven when she started to take me to the cinema. But mostly we were on our own. Kids were on their own. We were told to just leave the house and amuse yourselves. You were given a little bit of money and told to go and amuse yourself.

In Islington, there was an old fleapit cinema, the Blue Hall on Upper Street, just a bit further on from Angel, just past what is now Screen on the Green but which was called the Rex when I grew up. The Blue Hall was a classic

Little Fugitive

fleapit. It ran anything they could get their hands on that was cheap to run – second run, third run, fourth run. I remember I was aged ten and I went to see this film, *Little Fugitive*, which was a black-and-white film shot in Brooklyn about a little kid who ends up in Coney Island. It was so different to anything I had ever seen before. What I had seen before was either the very mediocre British movies or Hollywood movies. It was the very first film that was neither of those. It was a complete mistake, really, that I wandered in to see it. This fleapit running it wasn't an arthouse theatre or anything like that. They didn't exist in those days. I remember going to see this little film. It was the first film shot in a very naturalistic documentary style. It was the first film I had ever seen that wasn't manufactured to be a movie. I've looked it up since and I have seen quotes from Jean-Luc Godard and Truffaut saying it influenced that whole era of film-making, which at the time I had no knowledge of whatsoever.

The film was made in 1953. I would have seen it a good year or so later. I remember being completely and utterly mesmerised by it. It was a classic moment of going back to school and telling everybody about it. I always remember I had to stand up in class and talk about it. In my ignorance, I couldn't even pronounce the word fugitive because it is never said in the film. I remember standing up and I got a lot of laughs because I said I went to see this film, 'Little Fugg-itive'. 'Fugg-itive' sounded very rude. I was then put right by the teacher that it was actually pronounced 'fugitive'. It's an odd word, not a word that at ten I would have used in Islington.

The film was hugely influential. From then on, I went to see everything I could possibly see. Up to that point, cinema was just somewhere you went when you were bored. As regards to your brief, as regards to the epiphany moment, it undoubtedly was. Then, what happened almost immediately afterwards, and what I put into my documentary, *The Turnip's Head Guide to British Cinema*, I re-enacted the secondary moment which came after the epiphany moment. That was when I went to see a film called *The Sign of the Pagan* that starred Jack Palance as Attila the Hun and Jeff Chandler. But what I did when I came back to the school was to divide the whole playground into Romans and into Huns and then we had this entire battle. I got really told off for organising it but I wasn't organising it – I was actually

Sign of the Pagan
(Douglas Sirk,
1954)

directing it. It's the very earliest moment I can remember of me being bossy and telling people what to do. It was directed by Douglas Sirk who was thought to be a very journeyman Hollywood director but who was then discovered by the New Wave – the same people who had been influenced by this little documentary-drama *Little Fugitive*. In the space of six months, aged ten, I was influenced by both of these things.

It was probably another eight or ten years before I was aware or intelligent enough to realise what *Little Fugitive* was. It's not a great movie by any stretch of the imagination, but it is incredibly important in that at the moment it was made, it was unlike anything else that had been made. People have copied the technique since, which has become the whole thing of docudrama. But I remember I was fascinated by it because it didn't look like any Hollywood movie that I had been brought up on.

The film is very crudely shot. It was made by three people. One of them was Ruth Orkin, who was a very fine black-and-white photographer. It was obviously made by people used to doing documentaries. It's about a little boy in a working-class house in Brooklyn. The mother has to go away to look after her mother. She leaves behind the older brother, and the older brother is just pissed off because he has to look after little brother when he really wants to go with his pals to Coney Island. There is a scene in waste ground where the older brother and his friends pretend they've got a real gun and a real bullet and they give the little boy the gun. He fires the gun because he is obsessed with cowboys and Indians. He shoots it and the brother pretends to have been shot. The little boy is so distraught by this that he runs away. He doesn't know what to do. The mother left some money. He takes the money and he gets on the elevated railroad, which in those days went directly to Coney Island – Coney Island being like Southend-on-Sea or Blackpool or whatever.

At that time in the 50s, Coney Island was still very alive and busy. The film is his little journey, being lost in this world of grown-ups. He finally comes home and it ends quite happily. I suppose because the kid in the film was just about ten, or maybe a little younger, I identified with this little boy being alone without his family in a grown-up world in Coney Island. In those days, we thought nothing of getting on a train and going miles. Our parents didn't mind in those days. There was this whole thing of playing out on the streets. You wouldn't dream of your kids playing out there [now].

It was also to do with being introduced to an American world different to my own. I preferred the American films to the English films. *Little Fugitive* was an insight into American life that completely and utterly fascinated me. I remember thinking when he opened the fridge and took out a big bottle of milk to pour himself a glass, it was amazing. If I had helped myself to milk in my house, I would have been clipped around the ear because the milk was too precious. You weren't allowed it. You had a little bottle at school and that was it. That fascination with America came from that very moment. It was not this manufactured world of the Hollywood movie, which is what we had been fed, or the manufactured British films which were also kind of cardboard and very studio-based. It was the freedom of it, the looseness of it, the naturalness of it that impressed me so. I was never very fond of anything that was British. Remember, I came from Islington, a working-class background. The people in the English films didn't speak like us, anyway. They spoke in a very posh accent that had nothing to do with the world we lived in. If there was somebody trying to do a cockney accent, it was always totally naff. Somebody like Richard Attenborough pretending to be something he wasn't. They tended to be a lot of posh people in the British films. Or they were silly, like in the *Doctor* films.

I loved Norman Wisdom. I saw *Trouble in Store*, the very first one. That I saw with my mother. He used to sing in them. They were peculiar entertainments, really. He certainly wasn't Buster Keaton. But the fact it was in an English department store – I loved Norman Wisdom. And I can remember a film called *Hue and Cry*. I could identify with it because it was the same world I grew up in. I grew up in a world immediately after the Second World War in the centre of London where our playground, where I was brought up, was bombed ruins – the same place as that was set.

With *Little Fugitive*, it was a holiday and there was nothing else. Maybe we had already seen the Hollywood movie that was running at the Odeon or wherever. I remember I went with two friends from school. We wandered in. My friend Paddy Doolan whose dad ran the greengrocer said there was a film at the Blue Hall and we went to see it. I don't think they even stayed. They thought it was unbelievably boring. I remember they left. I was sat there in this Blue Hall cinema – it is not there any more – and there were only about half a dozen people in there anyway. Everybody left, including my two friends. I couldn't take my eyes off it. I saw it to the very end and I was the only one left sitting there.

When I got a bit older, by far the most influential film for me in a film-making sense was Ken Loach's *Cathy Come Home*, which was actually shown on television originally. I got hold of a 16mm print of it which I must have run about twenty times. That was a seminal film in my life without a doubt. It didn't just influence me. I think it influenced an entire generation of film-makers. That was back to the realism. It was not something that was made in a television studio, although it was made for television. It didn't have the cardboard sets of a *Play for Today* or the contrived silliness of the *Carry On* films. There is the most sensational moment which – to this day – is impossible to look at without being moved. That is where Carol White is sitting on a bench in a railway station and the welfare people arrive and take the children away from her. She is screaming. It is shot on a long lens. I think Ken Loach used her own children – so the kids were terrified. I don't know what it did to those kids.

Cathy Come Home
(Ken Loach, 1966)

It is a moment that is beyond cinema. It's real. It was all of Ken Loach. To me, he was the most influential. He was a director I could not wait to watch the films and I could not figure out how he did it. When I started to direct, he continued to baffle me with how brilliant he could be.

I didn't have any pretensions to be a film-maker until quite late. I was directing when I was twenty-four, which is not so late. I went into advertising. Out of that I was a copywriter. Then I started to direct commercials in the basement of the agency where we were. It was the beginnings of commercials in this country and we were allowed to experiment. It was a film school down in the basement of the agency, really. I started to make 30-second small films using all the people who worked in the agency. We would get the lady who worked in the accounts department or a chap who was quite chubby from the media department. I made about twenty of these little films in the basement, just experimenting, not really knowing what we were doing and not even really thinking at that point that I would be a director.

I wanted to be a writer more than anything else. I was writing in advertising and I was writing other things. But the

whole process of saying action and cut I hadn't even thought about. Somebody could work the tape recorder, somebody could work the camera, someone would edit it. They said, as you've written it, you better say 'action'. So I literally said action. That is how I became a director. I started to fix the performance. I started to get involved. I had written it and so I knew how I wanted it to be. Those commercials became more and more ambitious. We then had to make them for real so they could run on TV. Then it was suggested to me by the agency that perhaps I became a director. The first films we did won lots of awards. Obviously, we were quite good at it.

Charles Saatchi and David Puttnam were in the same agency. Charles wasn't interested in film at all and Puttnam was an account executive. It was the days of fantastic work in the press but nobody had really done commercials yet. At the time, the ambition was to get a double-page spread in *The Sunday Times* colour supplement. That was what everybody wanted to do.

I started doing commercials when I was twenty-three, twenty-four. By then, I had had a different education. I had had to catch up. I had started to go to the NFT and to arthouses. I had educated myself by then and, therefore, the

Brief Encounter or *Third Man*-type things we were doing pastiches of were used for what they were. We might not have had anything in common with them when they were around but suddenly we were looking back at them and using them as a device to sell Birds Eye dinners. These commercials were immaculately done with regards to attention to lighting, music, the quality of the acting. They were every bit as good as the originals. They just happened to be commercials. In fact, to make them as well as we possibly could showed we really thought they were significant. I really loved the photography of *Brief Encounter*. The first things we did, we were terrified. We were completely ignorant of what we were doing. And so the first thing you do is two people sitting at a table. You put the camera in front of it and you don't move it. And then, the second time, you do a commercial, you progress and you try to do other things. So I suddenly realised we could take people out onto the streets. You could have naturalistic dialogue. You didn't have to be somebody sitting in a very contrived set holding a packet of washing powder into the camera, which is what most commercials were when we first started. We were the first to produce miniature films as such. Then we got very ambitious. I remade *Brief Encounter* and anything that was going really. To be able to get the camera on the street – well, *Little Fugitive* had put into my head that film was more important than I had previously thought: what it could do and how you could express yourself.

Do I still have epiphanies? Once you start to do films as a feature-film director and you've got a few films under your belt, you start to be less impressed. When you start to see how to do it, you start to see the flaws in every film. Most film-makers would say that. I remember going to see *Raging Bull* and coming out and saying to another film-maker that it was very depressing because you think, one, I could never be as a good as that, or, two, maybe I could and therefore I have to try harder. A great movie for me now is when I don't think about why they are tracking, or why it is handheld, or why it is cut that way, or how stupid to run music under a serious dialogue scene. If I don't think about that at all and I am really, really absorbed by the film itself, then the film is really succeeding. **"**

Manoel De Oliveira

Berlin: Symphony of a City

(Walter Ruttmann, 1927)

Manoel De Oliveira is by some distance the oldest film-maker interviewed in this book. The Portuguese master was born in December 1908.

'I didn't celebrate my 100th birthday. Others celebrated it for me,' he told me of his centenary a few days after the birthday had fallen. 'I was very touched and moved by all the celebrations I was given by so many people this year. But I am not responsible for my age. It wasn't my decision to get to this age. It was a freak of nature that decided to allow me to live this long. I don't know how long it [my life] is going to last but hopefully for a long time. I am in no hurry to leave!'

I spoke to him in February 2009, in a suite in the Ritz Hotel in Berlin, just before the premiere of his latest feature, *Eccentricities of a Blond-Haired Girl*. He was a sprightly, humorous figure who looked considerably younger than his years. Oliveira was still working and was still impatient. It is often said about him that whereas his films unfold at a stately pace, he lives his life at top speed. In his younger years, Oliveira used to be a racing driver and he confides to me that when he first came to Berlin, it was to visit Mercedes to test out cars. 'These were the years of the beginning of the Hitler regime. I got here and the situation was really bad.'

A former acrobat as well as a racing driver, Oliveira is also an old-fashioned European intellectual. His documentary *Oporto of My Childhood* (2001) recounted a youth of theatregoing and intellectual debates in coffee houses … and of his early adventures in cinemagoing.

His choice of Walter Ruttmann's *Berlin: Symphony of a City* as his epiphany is in one way a surprise. It's a modernist documentary full of showy effects and far removed from his own work, which is known for its stately pace and lack of editing. However, in its celebration of speed, abstraction and the seething nature of city life, it evokes an earlier, more innocent time in film-making when the medium was slowly beginning to yield its secrets.

His father was a successful industrialist, and Oliveira attended school in Galicia, Spain. His initial ambition was to become an actor but he soon became fascinated by film directing. His first directorial effort was *Douro, Faina Fluvial* (1931). Over the next forty years, his film-making was sporadic. His first feature film, *Aniki-Bóbó* (1942), a portrait of Oporto's street children, wasn't especially well received. He re-emerged onto the film scene in 1956 with *The Artist and the City*, and followed this, in 1963, with *Acto de Primavera (The Rite of Spring)*, a documentary depicting an annual passion play. Bizarrely, Oliveira only really blossomed as a director in his eighties. Over the last twenty years, he has been extraordinarily prolific – and his work has regularly screened at Cannes, Venice and Berlin.

Manoel De Oliveira:

" I went to see movies first when I was five, six or seven years old with my father. I remember that one of the first movies I saw was a movie by Georges Méliès which I found very strange with those serpent-like figures. After that, I remember seeing a movie by Max Linder that I enjoyed very much and that made me laugh. Then, after that, I saw the movies by Charlie Chaplin. And I remember that when I went back home, I started acting myself, trying to imitate the actors I had seen on the screen.

I had no ambition or vocation to become a film-maker at the time. I thought maybe about becoming an actor but I was only seven years old. It was many years later, when I grew up, I remember seeing a movie that really impressed me. It was Walter Ruttmann's *Berlin: Symphony of a City*. That was a movie that really touched me very deeply and cleared up any doubts I might have had that I was going to become an author and a film-maker in the future.

At that time, it was very difficult to find a magazine or a book which managed to escape censorship about theories of montage. Ruttmann managed to elaborate an actual theory about montage (like those of Sergei Eisenstein or Dziga Vertov). In his case, it was in a chronological order, despite the speed of montage. His vision of editing was able to get to the essence of what was the situation at the time – to transfer the essence of the city of Berlin. It was a time when it was difficult to discover the theoretical part but we could see it in the movie.

That was a great time for editing. This has changed as our mentalities have changed, not only in cinema but in our lifestyles and in the way we 'live' our cities. What I liked about that style was the way it managed to progress, although it was able to retrieve the essential idea from the past. It had learned the idea of simplicity dating back to ancient Greece and the realism of the Italian renaissance. This is something that touches me today. Life is never stable. Life changes for all of us. A part of us keeps on changing with the passing of time. When we grow older, we change. It is as if we humans are always fighting against our own nature, which is always the same. There is this constant fight between our nature and our mind.

That film gave me the idea of making a symphony of Oporto, which was my home town. My father, as he would

always do, helped me. He brought me a Kinamo, a very small camera with 30mm film stock. It would allow 1-minute takes but not more than that. He also bought me the film stock to be able to shoot the movie. Luckily enough, I had met an old friend in the interval at a cinema screening. I had told him I intend to make a movie and he reached for a wallet in his pocket. He showed me he had become a very good photographer. At that point, I was unable to take any photographs. I knew nothing about photography. I told him I had the Kinamo camera and he is the one who taught me how to use it. After the movie, we created together a photography club.

Oporto is not a capital city. It's just a big port city. All of a sudden, I thought of this idea of a ship with a big anchor. This image led me to think about what was going to become my first movie, *Douro, Faina Fluvial*. At that point, I started dreaming about this movie, about this huge port with its docks, full of merchandise, big containers loaded and unloaded by big ships. It wouldn't have worked to have made a film in exactly the same style [as *Berlin: Symphony of a City*) but that was the starting point. **"**

Berlin: Symphony of a City

Don Boyd

Hamlet

(Laurence Olivier, 1948)

Scottish producer-director Don Boyd has enjoyed an extraordinarily varied career as a film-maker. He has produced Hollywood blockbusters and directed intimate documentaries; he has worked with avant-garde directors like Derek Jarman and has directed gangland yarns like the *King Lear*-influenced *My Kingdom* (2001). A networker extraordinaire, he has cultivated contacts in every different part of the British film industry. Critic Alexander Walker once called him 'a one-man film industry', a description that seems very apt given his remarkable facility for multitasking. Perhaps because his career has seemed to pull in so many different directions, his achievements haven't always been fully recognised, both for his own work as a director and in his capacity as an enabler of others.

Having graduated from the London Film School and worked on the BBC's science show *Tomorrow's World*, Boyd made his debut feature, *Intimate Reflections*, in 1975, about a couple mourning the death of their child. His second feature, *East of Elephant Rock* (1977), was a colonial drama set in Malaysia in 1948. Both films screened at the London Film Festival. At the same time as he was emerging as a film-maker, he was also one of the most dynamic and prolific producers in 1970s and 80s British cinema. His producer credits included Alan Clarke's *Scum* (1979), Derek Jarman's *The Tempest* (1979) and Julien Temple's *The Great Rock 'n' Roll Swindle* (1980) – all pivotal films of their era. As a contrast to this confrontational, lowish-budget work, he went on to produce John Schlesinger's $24 million *Honky Tonk Freeway* (1981). He also produced the portmanteau opera film *Aria* (1987), for which he assembled a small army of auteurs, among them Ken Russell, Jean-Luc Godard and Nic Roeg, to direct individual segments. Alongside his feature films, Boyd has directed many documentaries. He is a tireless lobbyist, promoting the activities of the Directors Guild of Great Britain. A true polymath, he was also a founding shareholder and director of Tartan Films, a leading UK arthouse distribution company. Boyd reached a huge TV audience through his work with comedienne Ruby Wax, whom he directed in a number of films, including one BAFTA-nominated portrait of Imelda Marcos. He is a Visiting Professor of Film at Exeter University. Meanwhile, he has a parallel career as a journalist, writing for such publications as the *Guardian*, *Observer* and *Time Out*.

Don Boyd:

" With the question of epiphany, if you're a purist, then there is one, like St Paul on the road to Damascus. In the case of one's passion in life, there are a plethora of epiphanies. It is rather like sex, in that you might have wonderful, passionate love-making with one woman and you think that there never could be better than that. Then something very different comes along which strikes you as being just as exciting. In that sense, sex and the cinema are rather similar to me, in that I have had massive moments in the cinema where I have felt that I have been experiencing a sort of extraordinary orgasm. Whether that is necessarily an epiphany or not, because one wonders to what extent that influences what you're going to do next and whether it influences your career path or your passions, I don't know. Certainly, in my case, it happened regularly.

My first really exciting moment came when I was living in east Africa. I was born in Scotland but my parents had lived all their early life in China. They came to Scotland to have me. Then, as soon as I was born, my father got a telegram saying the communists have moved into Shanghai, which is where they were living, and could he move to Hong Kong. I went straight back to Hong Kong. From then onward, I lived in Hong Kong, Uganda and Kenya. While I did that, I went to a Scottish school called Loretto.

When I was in east Africa, I was taken to this extraordinary event – extraordinary for a variety of reasons, not least that the group I was part of were the only whites among about 5,000 Africans. I remember it was a very, very dusty, parched environment. We had to sit on a surface called murram, which was red parched earth. There was no grass. I remember being very excited about my trousers getting dirty as a result. A truck arrived. I remember watching all of this. My father must have been vaguely involved in the set-up. A large sheeting of white was draped over a makeshift scaffolding and the back of the truck had a projector. It must have been a 35mm projector. Makeshift speakers were put out. The light disappeared quickly on the Equator. Within 25 minutes, it was dark. Over a period of about half an hour, suddenly it was dark and on came first the cockerel of British Movietone news. I don't remember the item but it was a news programme of some kind. That was followed by some kind of short –

probably something like Edgar Lustgarten. It was a silly little thriller. Then came on the reason why we were there, which was Laurence Olivier's *Hamlet*. It was in black and white. I still have that image of Laurence Olivier delivering 'to be or not to be' as he is looking down on the waves, from the rampart of Elsinore.

I was completely blown away by what seemed to me very poetic, beautiful language. I was not familiar with the play because my parents were not in any way cultural. My father was in the tobacco business and had had intelligence connections in the war and had worked for MI5. His 'front' job was working for BAT. He was totally non-cultural. My mother was Russian. Shakespeare, Dickens – all those things – I had to read later on. I didn't know very much about those things. I was hearing poetic English coming from those actors and I also realised that this was not something that was like the theatre. It was moving locations. There were realistically portrayed scenes which struck me as being an approximation of what might have been happening in real terms.

The camera was moving. The photographic imagery I was unfamiliar with because I hadn't been exposed to that

Hamlet

form of poetic and well-lit photographic image. That, combined with sitting around these people whose first language was Swahili – their African tongue – and seeing these people spontaneously applaud imagery and speeches given in a language they didn't understand. And yet, they seemed to get what was going on. Obviously, the cheering and applause came during the sword fight. They seemed to understand who was good and bad.

I can't have been any older than about six or seven. I remember feeling this is so exciting – to be watching something being projected, hearing the whirr from some machine onto a screen. At the end of it, I said to my dad, how did that machine produce those images? He didn't know. I said I want to do that. I want to be able to make what that is and be as excited by it as other people. Very shortly afterwards, I won a scholarship with some money. He [my father] bought me a Johnsons of Hendon developing outfit and a camera. It was actually a very good camera, an AGFA flip-flop camera – a small bellows camera. He said learn how to take pictures with this. That was about the only educational input my father ever had for me. From then on, I hardly saw him after I went to

school. He was never particularly close to me. But that he did do. I began to take black-and-white pictures with a 120 film. I began to do that before I went to school. When I went to school, I knew how to use a darkroom. They had a darkroom there that I could use. There was a direct link between the epiphany of this experience of watching Olivier and of watching this film, being excited by it in this very bizarre, Salvador Dali-like landscape and feeling that I absolutely had to be able to create that form of magical experience. My dad was clever enough to realise that I was exceptionally serious about this. The only other passion we had for ourselves until then, my brother and I, was a passion connected with rugby. He [my father] loved rugby and he wanted me to play for Scotland. The two things I remember him giving me of any symbolic value were a rugby ball and this Johnsons of Hendon kit and camera with a couple of rolls of 120 film, and that led to my passion from then onward. The enthusiasm from that period was compounded when, at prep school, we saw films on 16mm. They were the films you'd expect us to see at a posh boarding school – *Bridge on the River Kwai*, *I'm Alright Jack* – nothing of any great social consequence. *Bridge on*

the River Kwai was a wonderful movie and I really enjoyed seeing it but I wouldn't say I came away from it with any sense of epiphany. I already had got the bug and understood it. My brother also won a scholarship and with that money we bought a little 8mm movie camera and we made a film of our own.

The second epiphany came to me later on, when I left school, very young, very qualified, aged sixteen. I was too young to go to university but was qualified enough to do so. I said to my father that I wanted to go to work with actors. He said if you're going to do that, you'll have to do it yourself. I was living in Edinburgh and had to come down to London for an audition to drama school. During that era, I don't remember where but I think it was the Cameo cinema in Edinburgh, I saw Pasolini's *Gospel According to St. Matthew*. That film – which I saw again at film school – was an epiphany. I had become extremely radical politically. I had had a very, very High Church upbringing which was compounded at Loretto, where they allowed both the High Church service and the Low Church service to crop up. The High Church involved the rituals but also the musical tradition. I couldn't square that religious influence with my

Gospel According to St. Matthew (Pier Paolo Pasolini, 1964)

sense of what politics might be about. This was during the 60s when there was a huge amount of political alteration and social change. This showed me Christ as the ordinary man. It showed it in such a poetic way with moving cameras. It presented a set of circumstances I could identify with. Although this was a construct, it was one I could believe. Pasolini conveyed to me and to many others who saw the film this sense that Christ had, in his own extraordinary, revolutionary way, a Marxist agenda or an agenda that was approximated in the socio-economic tracks of people like Engels and Marx. I was never a communist and disapproved of that. I had my mother's influence. She was Russian, brought up in China and was fearfully anti-communist and for huge reason. She lost her brother in the Stalin era. But I was massively influenced by the left-wing political movement.

Pasolini's film blew my mind. I realised there was an opportunity to use cinema in a way that was beyond the straightforward commercial entertainment. That might have been a ruinous epiphany. From then on, I wanted to make sure that whatever I did was worth the time because it felt that you only had a finite time. In all my choices,

I have always remembered that influence … and the influence of people who were watching images in a language that isn't their own, that those Africans applauded and cheered when they didn't really have a clue.

Years later, I was able to tell Laurence Olivier the story [about the screening in Africa] myself. I produced some of the work of Derek Jarman. We'd made *The Tempest* and *The Last of England*. He had a notion about Benjamin Britten. I said let's do *War Requiem* as a movie. I quite amazingly managed to persuade Laurence Olivier to be in the opening section of the film. It was the last thing he did. He died in the April and we shot in the September and October before that. It was released on the 1 January of the year he died. I had been lucky enough to work with Lindsay Anderson and he was inspirational in showing you how you deal with actors. He was so good at that, so direct. There was no woolliness. He was specific and forthright. Olivier invited us to his home. Everybody had thought he was senile but he became articulate. He also had an amazing memory. When I told him the story about the *Hamlet*, he redid the soliloquy for me in his home. The epiphany came when we started talking about technique. I said is there something special you do that has made you one of the great actors of all time. He did two things that made me understand an actor in a way I had never done before. He said it was all technique. When we were leaving the house, he tapped Derek on the shoulder, said I've got something for you. Derek said oh, what can that be? He went off, shuffled away and came back with a pair of shoes and said you're going to need these. They were big shoes. And, yes, of course, they were needed because Derek needed the shoe size and kind of shoe for the clothing that he was going to be wearing in the film. It was a detail thing. **"**

Lord David Puttnam

Pinocchio

(Walt Disney, 1940)

David Puttnam is as close as contemporary British cinema has come to a Michael Balcon figure. Like the old Ealing Studios boss, he is a patrician figure who sees cinema as a way to inspire and educate as well as to entertain. Films with which Puttnam is associated – among them *Chariots of Fire* (1981), *The Mission* (1986), *The Killing Fields* (1984) and *Memphis Belle* (1990) – all had a crusading zeal about them. In his pomp as a producer, he was an advocate of what might best be described as intelligent populism – he didn't make popcorn movies.

Born in 1941, Puttnam came into British film-making via advertising. By the time of *Chariots of Fire* in 1981, he was the most recognisable film producer in Britain. Audiences may not have been able to identify just who directed *Stardust* (1974) or *That'll Be the Day* (1973) or even *Chariots of Fire* itself, but most knew the name of the bearded man with the flowing hair who had helped usher these movies into existence. Puttnam flourished at a time when British cinema was in the doldrums. Audiences had collapsed, cinemas were in a state of disrepair, production funding was hard to access and new talent wasn't emerging. Against such a backcloth, he seemed almost like a Messiah figure, working with Goldcrest and giving opportunities to directors like Alan Parker, Bill Forsyth and Roland Joffe. Puttnam was prepared to make films of scale – the kinds of movies that could reach international audiences and win major awards.

Puttnam's sheer zeal and enthusiasm couldn't help but catch the eye of Hollywood. In 1986, he was recruited to head up Columbia Pictures by the studio's then owners, Coca-Cola. It proved an unhappy posting. The stealth and machiavellianism required to thrive in Hollywood didn't come naturally to Puttnam. He was considered priggish and self-righteous. The Hollywood insiders closed ranks against him and his well-intentioned efforts to reform the excesses of the studio system came to nothing. His stint as a studio boss lasted only a year.

Back in Britain in the 1990s, Puttnam became increasingly involved in politics and education. He withdrew from active film production. Nonetheless, his influence behind the scenes hadn't diminished. Whether it was to do with how National Lottery money should be spent on film or through his work as Chairman of the National Film and Television School, he was (and remains) a pivotal figure in UK film culture.

David Puttnam:

" The first epiphany without doubt was when I saw *Pinocchio*, aged seven or eight. It was in 1948. I was taken by my aunt who (ironically) happened to be a film editor at Kays' Labs – a film cutter, a negative cutter. I absolutely distinctly remember walking out of the cinema and across the foyer, thinking that's what I want to do, and I didn't even know what 'that's what I want to do' meant. I wanted to do whatever it was that made me feel what I had just felt. I had no way of being more tangible about it than that. I just felt fantastic. I felt I had been taken into another world and I suppose I realised I had been manipulated. I didn't know if that meant I wanted to be an animator. It would have been the Wood Green Odeon. The first three films that I saw were all cartoons. My mother only took me to see cartoons. I didn't know there was anything but cartoons. For me, cinema was cartoons. A while later, I saw my first live-action film with human beings in it. That [*Pinocchio*] was the first epiphany. It was a long, circuitous route. I didn't end up producing my first film until I was twenty-nine.

My father was a photographer, which meant I was a little more sophisticated than the average kid in that I had been brought up in a very visually literate family. I only met my dad when I was five and he came back from the war and immediately went back to Fleet Street. There was a sense that photographs were very important. He had stacks and stacks of his own photographs at home. I used to go sifting through them as a kid. I knew that film was a manufactured product but I could lose myself in it at the same time. I knew it was also something far more sophisticated than what I had been accustomed to with my dad. I remember the feeling. I was in the foyer. There was a lot of chatter going on. My aunt Olive said to me, did you enjoy that? Enjoy that, I said – that's what I want to do.

I was brought up during the war. My world was a world of allotments, walking to school. Looking back, we lived in a very small house but a very cosy house, and I had a mum who was obsessively concerned with me. I spent three years sleeping in an air-raid shelter. You forget things like that. I was evacuated for six months to Droitwich. We stayed with a family over a greengrocer's shop. I've never even been back to Droitwich!

I started going to the cinema regularly with my mother. That was at the Southgate Odeon. It was a little later. I was probably around ten. Then I started going to Saturday-morning pictures. That was again at the Southgate Odeon.

Then, I was very lucky. By the time I was twelve, I was able to walk to five different cinemas. That was extraordinary. Now, we're in 1952, '53 and '54. I was lyrical about Ealing but the truth was my first choice every week would be the Technicolor film. I'd go to the colour film. Then I might go to the one I'd seen on the trailer. More often than not, it was the third film that was the British film. My relationship with British films was something of an embarrassment to me when I became very friendly with Michael Balcon in later years. I guess I was the British film-makers' nightmare because I went to British films when I had run out of American films to see. I remember seeing those British films but they were incidental to the main meal.

At that point, I loved Technicolor movies. I loved musicals. I liked Westerns. I knew enough then to know that I preferred Gary Cooper to Anthony Steel. He was much more cool. And [I liked] Jimmy Stewart and Gregory Peck. I remember being hugely impressed by Gregory Peck in *Horatio Hornblower*. I thought he was the greatest thing. A little later, the next actor who hit me through the eyes and a film that had a huge impact on me was a film that is quite hard to find now, with Montgomery Clift – *The Search*. It's Fred

Zinnemann's first film. It is set in Austria immediately after the war. A GI [played by Montgomery Clift] very reluctantly becomes caught up with an orphan kid, who he doesn't really want to look after but he starts looking after. Funnily enough, if you shot it today, people would immediately think paedophilia. One thing leads to another and he starts to look for the child's mother. Aline MacMahon plays the nurse who is the head of the hospital he took the kid to – the orphanage. At the end of a very good film, they find the mother. It's a very interesting film because it was co-financed by MGM and the UN – maybe the only film that ever was. It was trying to establish what the United Nations was doing in Europe for orphans and child resettlement. That film had a massive effect on me. Ironically, I am now President of Unicef and I honestly believe there to be a direct relationship between that and my seeing that film, being affected by that film, knowing that it was about this United Nations organisation which changed its name. I wanted to be Montgomery Clift. I wanted to be that GI. That was the first time I had totally identified with an individual.

I loved the Western or the musical. I loved Gene Kelly. Then, suddenly, this

Pinocchio

East of Eden
(Elia Kazan,
1954)

film came along. It was made in '48. I saw it in '52 or '53, so certainly in re-release. I would have seen it at the Queens, Palmers Green. That was a re-release house. It was probably the third film I saw that week and it just happened to be that one.

Hard on the back of that, within eighteen months, James Dean came into my life. That was a huge thing because what James Dean was was the very, very first person who articulated a kind of unease. What happened in the mid-50s was a disconnection between the adult world and the teen world. You knew it had happened. We weren't American – we were probably a couple of years behind America. You look at *Rebel without a Cause* and no one I knew had a car. You couldn't identify really with *Rebel without a Cause*. I literally didn't know anyone who had a car. But what you did identify with was the confusion and angst. For me, it was more so in *East of Eden*. That was a fantastically important film for me, partly because I was absolutely devoted to my dad. The resolution at the end of *East of Eden* was tremendously important to me because it said to me that you could have a real problem with your parents. You could have a real problem with your father. Then, there was this marvellous scene at the end where the father has had the stroke and ends up depending on him [Dean]. That was sort of an epiphany in terms of self-discovery.

The next epiphany was in the 1960s, seeing *The Battle of Algiers*. It just hit me between the eyes. I suddenly realised that film was something quite other. It could have another whole purpose, another whole role. A lot of my work is absolutely the child of *The Battle of Algiers*. I saw it at the NFT. When I was seventeen, I had got a job at an ad agency. I was a tennis player. I played tennis very seriously. The only place, believe it or not, where you could play tennis in London was at two sunken courts right next door to the NFT, just along where the old pleasure gardens had been. I had that booked, I think it was every Thursday evening. I was at night school two nights a week. I used to play there. And we used to finish there at 7pm and go to the NFT. That was where I saw *The Battle of Algiers*.

I had a pen pal who was French Algerian. We used to write to each other, so I knew a little bit more about that than the normal eighteen- or nineteen-year-old would have done. Then I had suddenly lost touch with him. I knew he had gone into the army and I knew what was going on. He was in the FLN [the National Liberation Front] and he had written to me. So I had a bit of

*The Battle of
Algiers* (Gillo
Pontecorvo, 1966)

background [about Algeria]. Then there was this thing of watching this movie and not really realising what I was watching, until I realised the camera was inside the cave. I thought, hang on a second, the camera is in there. This is not a documentary. This is real. I was very confused by the film. I found the torture scenes just killed me. If any film really was an epiphany, it was *The Battle of Algiers* for me. I reeled out of the cinema a changed person. I was confused. It had made me completely rethink what cinema was. To me, it has been first of all an entertainment medium. It was a medium which allowed me to deal with some of my childhood angst and ambitions. But this was something else. This was politics. It politicised me.

The first time I went to America was in 1964 for my job. For me, that was going home. My home was there. My cinematic home was there, my romantic home was there and my emotional home was there. I really consciously remember coming to land in New York being like coming home.

When I made *Midnight Express* here [in the UK], that was a job when I realised this wasn't why I had come into the film industry. I remember having an argument with Alan Parker about it and he was cross with me. *Midnight Express* was

a very well-made film. It was very successful. It wasn't what I wanted to do.

Chariots of Fire was in a sense a deliberate act of defiance. *Chariots of Fire*, all that part of my work, *The Mission*, all grew out of the next film that had a big impact on me – *Lawrence of Arabia*. That did knock me out. That pulled everything together. The politics, the scale – it all fitted in an odd way. I saw *The Battle of Algiers* before I saw *Lawrence of Arabia*. It would have been interesting to see what happened if I saw them the other way round. The night before we started shooting *Chariots of Fire*, Hugh Hudson and I showed *Lawrence* to the cast. The reason we showed it to them was that while people think of it as an epic of landscapes, it is actually a film of close-ups. If you really analyse it, it's a film of that. Time and time again, you are on those eyes, that face. That was one of the things we wanted to show to them. In a sense, it was almost a sleight of hand. The epic quality never took away from the humanity. The film was always about a man. I didn't respond to O'Toole in the way I had to James Dean or Montgomery Clift. That had been about identity. That was me finding out who I was and evolving an identity out of Monty Clift and James Dean. By the time I saw *Lawrence of Arabia*, I think I knew who I was. **"**

Frank Darabont

THX 1138

(George Lucas, 1971)

Frank Darabont has not made many features. However, his 1994 film *The Shawshank Redemption*, which he adapted from a story by Stephen King, has long been acknowledged as a contemporary classic – a film that continues to sell in huge numbers on DVD, is often revived and scores highly on lists of the top films of all time. A prison drama with an unlikely emotional depth and with exceptional performances from Tim Robbins and Morgan Freeman, it was a movie that performed in only mediocre fashion on its initial release but that was slowly lifted by word of mouth, eventually becoming a full-blown phenomenon. The film has been ranked as No. 1 on IMDb's top 250 films of all time and has also featured on the 2007 American Film Institute list of the top 100 films of all time.

Darabont and his family came to the US after his parents fled Hungary following the 1956 uprising. 'I was an infant when we arrived in the US,' he recalls. 'I was not actually born in Hungary. My parents had already fled. I was born in a refugee camp in France in 1959, three years after the uprising. We came over on the boat. They [my parents] were carrying me in a picnic basket. They were bringing me, my brother and the clothes on their back.'

Darabont's family eventually ended up in Los Angeles. While studying at Hollywood High School, he began to become obsessed by cinema. Rather than go to college, he embarked on his film-making career working as a crew member on low-budget movies. In 1983, he made his first short, *The Woman in the Room*. Like much of his subsequent work, including *The Shawshank Redemption*, this was based on a story by horrror writer Stephen King. Eventually, Darabont became established as a screenwriter, having scripted horror movies like *The Blob* (1988) and *The Fly II* (1989).

There was a five-year hiatus between *The Shawshank Redemption* and Darabont's well-received *The Green Mile* (1999). He has not been as prolific as might have been expected in the wake of the successes of these two films. Nonetheless, he remains in demand as a writer (working as a script doctor on some very high-profile movies, among them *Saving Private Ryan*, 1998, and *Minority Report*, 2002) and has continued to adapt King's work for the screen, most recently with *The Mist* (2007).

Frank Darabont:

" Epiphanies? I may have a good answer for you. Those epiphanies come in layers, over periods of time. You'll wind up seeing *It's a Wonderful Life* on television as a child and it just wrecks you, or *Sunset Boulevard* – the first time I saw that, I saw it on a big screen at a revival house when I was younger and was floored by it. I remember sitting in a theatre as a child and seeing Stanley Kubrick's *2001*, having no clue at the time what I was seeing but loving it – those things do accrue. But I remember very, very distinctly that I had one experience at the age of twelve. I loved horror movies and I had gone to see this low-budget horror movie called *The Brotherhood of Satan*. Playing as a second feature with *The Brotherhood of Satan* was this very obscure first movie from a young director called *THX 1138*. That would be the greatest epiphany for me. I remember being in the theatre. In fact, I sat through it twice. I sat through *Brotherhood of Satan* again so I could see *THX* again. It was the real cognisance I had that there was an artist behind the camera – that there was a film-maker at work, pulling the strings, making this happen and sharing with the audience his worldview, which was stamped on every frame of that film. It was a breath-taking thing. When you're a kid, movies just happen. They're spontaneous magic. You don't really think about actually making or crafting a film on an intellectual level. That is the film where it suddenly occurred to me – aha! – there are people who actually do this. I remember walking out of the theatre and really wanting to be that guy [the director]. It informed me that cinema at its best is a form for self-expression.

Sadly, as a caveat to this, I should say that the version of *THX 1138* that now exists on DVD is not the version that I saw in the theatre when I was twelve years old. George [Lucas] has seen fit for reasons beyond me, which I don't understand, to add a bunch of CGI to it, which I think works against the beautiful, spare Japanese aesthetic that he had struck upon when he had first made it. To me, it's a very confused and schizophrenic film now. There was a great purity to what had been there before. And by the way, I have bought the laser disc of it and watched it again not that long ago because the original version of the movie is on laser disc. But you need a laser player. And that's like saying you need an 8-track player. They're almost impossible to get – I bet they're out there on eBay!

I loved the confusion of the people [in *THX*] living in this culture wherein they had become mere cogs in a system. That is always a fantastic observation to make. It hasn't been made enough and I don't think it was ever made better than in George's original film – trying to find some identity, individuality, moral clarity. It's surprising, watching it now as an adult, how much of it I understood at the age of twelve, but I did. I apparently left nothing on the table when I saw that movie. I got it all. I loved that films could be philosophical like that. Ultimately, it's a very unique and distinct film, compelled by the fact he had a very low budget. There was a need for some very clever, inventive solutions, one of the most striking of which is the prison environment, where they hold the undesirables and the political prisoners. Well, you don't have money to build a set – let's make it a white void! I thought, my God, that's brilliant, really. It's the kind of solution that springs from a fertile mind in a film-school kind of environment – how to make the most with the least. Sometimes, those solutions can be incredibly exciting because it is using the lens to great effect, showing you something you've never seen before. It's not just a budgetary compromise – it is a marvellous creative choice.

THX 1138

That's one of the reasons why I am so disappointed George decided to throw all this money into it and do this bloody CGI.

I am certain there is a kinship between *THX* and my own work in *Shawshank Redemption*. They're both about people lost in a system, trying to find their way and get out. But all those films that inspired us when we were growing up and at a certain age – little bits of that leak into the work, sometimes in incredibly subtle ways. It can be the choice of a music cue, for example, in *The Green Mile* that I can trace directly back to *The Abominable Dr Phibes*, another film I saw when I was twelve.

I had discovered cinema myself. My father was unsympathetic. Why? Because he was a dick, an asshole. This is not an opportunity to sit down on the couch and tell you about my dad but we did not get along well. In one sense, cinema was the escape for me. It was the way to experience lives that were quite different from my own and learn things about the world. For me, it became a very solitary pursuit. I was always haunting the revival houses back then, pre-video of course, and seeing everything I could. The volume of things being released back then was far

less. I can't imagine trying to see every-thing now that comes out but I was cer-tainly trying to do that when I was younger. And I was exploring the past as well, going to the revival houses to see *Stalag 17* or *Slaughterhouse-Five* or *The General*. That was just as fantastic for me as anything contemporary. I was always fascinated and interested – and still am – by what has come before, even the language of cinema and how you see it developing as an art form.

Where did I see *THX*? It had to have been Los Angeles. Given it was a double bill with *Brotherhood of Satan*, it couldn't have been a particularly posh theatre. It had to have been one of those second-run things. The fact that *THX* was the second feature showed you how badly it was released by Warner Bros. of the day. They just appended it to a low-budget horror movie and tossed it out there.

I really don't remember where the theatre was. I remember the experience of being at the theatre all day long, then going home and my mother wondering where I had been.

The other epiphany was Stephen King. The very first Stephen King thing I had done was a little thing [a short adaptation of King's *The Woman in the Room*] that I had done when I was twenty. I see nothing but flaws with it

now, although Steve liked it well enough and when I reapproached him some years later for the rights to *Shawshank*, he was very happy to give them to me. Really, my interest in King I trace back to my high-school days when the book of *The Shining* came out. That book fell into my hands purely by accident. It was mis-shipped to me by the book club. I didn't really have any money at the time. I didn't think I would buy the book because I couldn't afford it. I pulled it out of the box and looked at it. I didn't know who the hell this guy was, this Stephen King. But the book looked intriguing and I opened it and read one page. Then I said to myself, I've got to keep the book. I've got to find the money. Instantly, I was captivated by it. *The Shining* was my first introduction to King and I became a constant reader from that point on, exploring everything that he had published. I think it is fair to categorise reading *The Shining* as an epiphany. It made me a lifelong devotee of King's work.

You can't really replicate the experi-ence of falling into the pages of a book. Most reading experiences are simply reading experiences, even the good ones, but there are the rare ones that absolutely suck you into the pages of a book. The story becomes more real to you than the life that surrounds you. You can't put the damned thing down. That's the hallmark of a really great work.

King's storytelling was tremendously humanistic, tremendously rooted in character, tremendously compelling stuff. Ultimately, he has got such a great imagination when it comes to plot mechanisms and the surrounding furniture of a story. Where his work really lives, the beating heart of it, is this fantastic facility with characters. It's not unlike Dickens that he just gets you so married to his characters that you must go along on the journey. He is a remarkable man for that. The successful films, the ones that people point to and say that's a good Stephen King adaptation, tend to be the ones that didn't forget that, whether it's *Stand by Me*, *Dolores Claiborne* or *The Dead Zone* or *Misery*. Those were the ones that knew why the story was great – because of the characters. The ones that failed forgot … they didn't think that that [the characterisation] was the important stuff. They thought it was the surrounding furniture. That has led to some not too good adaptations.

With George [Lucas], I had a working relationship that spanned some years and didn't end up in a happy place. But that's OK. With Steve [King], he just turned into a really good friend. He has been a friend and a supporter from the get-go. It is interesting to meet a man like him. He is so damned good. He can be so sophisticated in his writing but when you meet him, he's just a sweet, goofy guy. He'll chatter away with you. Everything he says is interesting but you wouldn't necessarily think great writer when you meet him. He doesn't have the pretension at all. He knows the value of his work and his efforts. Some he is prouder of than others but he is not full of himself in any way, shape or form. He is still living in the place where he grew up. He didn't move to LA or the South of France. He is just who he is.

As a movie-lover, I can only liken the continuing success of *Shawshank Redemption* to those films I keep being drawn back to, whether it's *Sunset Boulevard* or *Almost Famous*. There is something about the storytelling that people want to revisit. I am very flattered to be in company like that. **"**

Lars von Trier

Barry Lyndon

(Stanley Kubrick, 1975)

Lars von Trier on
the set of *The
Element of Crime*
(1984)

Given his reputation, von Trier is a surprisingly friendly and unaffected man. The founder of Dogme 95 and one of European cinema's most maverick and controversial figures, the middle-aged Dane has a reputation as an agent provocateur. At the time I meet him, he has just finished filming a comedy, *The Boss of It All* (2006), for which the camera was controlled by computer.

Some US critics were scandalised by his minimalist films *Dogville* (2003) and *Manderlay* (2005), which were accused of being anti-American. The low-budget Dogme doctrine that he largely evolved has been a source of both inspiration and huge annoyance to film-makers and audiences. Nonetheless, thanks to its success, and to the brilliance of such earlier films as *Breaking the Waves* (1996) and *The Kingdom* (1994), von Trier has managed the unlikely feat (for a Danish film director who doesn't like flying) of making himself an international figure. He is the one Danish director that everybody has heard of.

Over lunch, he is hospitable and easygoing. This, he reveals, is not necessarily because he likes visitors but because he believes that countries are judged by how they react to outsiders. It is not long since the Danish cartoon scandals (when satirical cartoons published in a Danish newspaper caused huge offence in the Muslim world and provoked a bitter debate within Denmark about immigration and tolerance). At a time when some in his country are becoming far more hostile to outsiders, von Trier has made it a point of principle to treat any non-Danes with extra hospitality and respect.

The Boss of It All suggested a new mellowness in von Trier. He was in his fifties when he made it and claimed that he was now going to take stock of his life. Rather than bring the film to Cannes, he premiered it in more modest fashion in Copenhagen. Nonetheless, the idea that von Trier was somehow softening was thrown into stark relief by his next film, *Antichrist* (2009). This film – dedicated to Russian master Andrei Tarkovsky – managed to provoke the critics all over again. When it premiered in Cannes, it actually received an 'anti-award', so disgusted were the ecumenical jury members by its perceived misogyny and nihilism.

Lars von Trier:

"Epiphanies? There are many. The Andrei Tarkovsky films had a big influence. I started seeing them when I was at film school. Maybe I had seen some before but I saw *Mirror* at film school and that was a revelation to me. There are certain points in your life when you are very open to things. Now, I would consider myself to be very closed in terms of finding the film that I would learn from but, at this time, I saw *Mirror* and later on I saw *Stalker*. He has had a tremendous influence on me, Tarkovsky. There are a few wow films and *Mirror* is definitely one of them. It was mostly about these shots of this cabin in the woods. All the trees, wind and whatever. The strange way people act in these films is more like a dream feeling. I saw these tracking shots in and around the house in the woods and it just appealed to me somehow. It was all very strange. Nobody has ever really been able to say what the film is about! But I like strange films, mysteries. I like the poetry also of the film. I think Tarkovsky was helped quite a lot by being in the Soviet Union. First of all, he could do these films that nobody would have done because they couldn't finance them – he financed them somehow. They say that *Stalker* is very much a criticism of the Soviet Union and its politics. I am not so fond of the films Tarkovsky made when he came to Europe. *Solaris*, *Mirror* and *Stalker* were the three films I liked the most. The other students thought it was strange. I can only say that I like it very much. I'll stop anything just to see half an hour of this film.

And *Barry Lyndon* and *The Deer Hunter*. These films are somehow monumental. They are long but they are very clear in style. Watching *Barry Lyndon* is a pleasure, like eating a very good soup. It is very stylised and then suddenly comes some emotion [when the child falls off the horse]. There's not a lot of emotion. There are a lot of moods and some fantastic photography, really like these old paintings. Thank God he didn't have a computer. If he had a computer at that time, you wouldn't care but you know he has been waiting three weeks for this mountain fog or whatever. It's overwhelming with the boy because it is suddenly this emotional thing. The character Barry Lyndon is not very emotional. In fact, he's the opposite. He's an opportunist.

I saw the film when it came out. I was in my early twenties. The first time I saw it, I slept. It was on too late and it's a very, very long film. What is interesting is that Nicole Kidman told me Kubrick hated long films. If you've seen

Barry Lyndon

the last scene of the film, where she is writing out a cheque for him, it's extremely long. It goes on and on and on but it's beautiful. The good thing is that Kubrick always sets his standards. *Barry Lyndon* to me is a masterpiece. He casts in a very strange way, Kubrick. It is a very strange cast. But that is how the film should be, of course. This thing that he liked short films was very surprising. And he liked Kieślowski very much. He was crazy about Kieślowski.

I don't know if Kubrick saw any of my films but I know Tarkovsky watched the first film I did and hated it! That's how it is supposed to be. The narration in *Manderlay* and *Dogville* is definitely inspired by *Barry Lyndon* and the narration there – this ironical voice, this whole chapter thing, the feeling there are chapters. I've done that in *Dogville* and *Manderlay* and to some extent in *Breaking the Waves*. It's all Kubrick!

Carl Dreyer's *Gertrud* was another film. I saw that before film school, ten years ago, I had thought about making a documentary on *Gertrud*. The problem is that all these people have died, all the people who worked on *Gertrud*. The point I wanted to make, if I was going to do something on *Gertrud*, was that everybody – the crew and actors – were so evil to Dreyer. They thought he was

too much of an artist and that the film was going to be really awful. It was the last film he did. From the interviews I did, just talking to people, they were extremely cruel to this old man who had made a lot of good films. They were making fun of him and they thought it was ridiculous what they were doing. I saw it in a cinema. I saw all the Dreyer films and all the Bergman films. I had been studying films at university. I just saw in the paper today that Bergman said *Fanny and Alexander* was inspired by *Dallas*. He says that in his diary. Maybe if he had said that before, I could have seen it with more pleasure. I was not especially fond of *Fanny and Alexander*. I was very fond of the old Bergman films.

I started making 8mm films when I was ten or eleven. My mother had a camera but she didn't know how to use it. It was old-fashioned, before the light meter and stuff. You had to be a little technical to use it. I learned by trying it out – and by reading the manual. That's a good start. I made feature films straight away, little feature films. I always liked the technical side of films – dollies and cranes, all the technical side. I did a lot of technical stuff with this 8mm camera – double exposure, fades in and out, strange lighting effects. I used indoor film outdoors and vice versa to see what

Mirror (Andrei
Tarkovsky, 1974)

strange colours I could get out of that. You could cheat by using this different stock material. They were very cheap. I think my mother financed them. Later on I did 16mm films and I had to work to finance them. I was making feature films of an hour. One was very inspired by *The Story of O*. But that was when I was at the university, when I was twenty, not when I was eleven. There was no S&M, not an obvious level, in the 8mm films.

One of the other films was about somebody who had seen a car accident. One of the spectators fled into the woods and tried to get away. Another was about a man or boy who planted a flower and kept it from all the cruelty of the world. I showed them only to my friends. They were feature films. They had a name. I had a fantastic projector with sound on it. You could put a little soundtrack onto the film. You could put a lot of sound and music and sound effects.

My uncle was a film-maker. He made documentaries. My mother supported it [my film-making] very much. I made a lot of cartoons or parts of cartoons. We were sitting and painting and drawing on cellophane. It was a small industry but the film was never finished. All the technique actually fascinated me from the beginning.

I read a small thing that Stephen King had been writing about Kubrick and *The Shining* and had claimed Kubrick had no idea of how to frighten people. There is an example where Shelley Duvall comes out where he has been writing 'all work makes Jack a dull boy'. I was kind of disappointed when I first saw *The Shining* because it was just after *Barry Lyndon* but it is a good film. I think maybe the more scary side of it – maybe it's more women who find it scary but it's a beautiful film. This whole hotel that has its own life. I liked *Eyes Wide Shut*. I am a Kubrick man but I've only seen it two times, so I should maybe see it again. There are some things in it that stay with you. I was not so crazy about *Clockwork Orange*, the absurdity of it. I liked *Barry Lyndon* and *2001* the most. They were more serious. *Barry Lyndon* for me was by far the greatest. Everything was right.

At one stage, I wanted to make a series called 'Films that made me make films', with a commentary on the whole film. We couldn't finance it. I thought it was a good idea. I would love to see Scorsese if he had to choose five films and make a commentary. For me, there was *Gertrud*, there was *Barry Lyndon* and there was *Mirror*. ❞

Atom Egoyan

Persona

(Ingmar Bergman, 1966)

Canadian director Atom Egoyan first sprang to prominence in the 1980s with his disquieting films about voyeurism and video technology *Next of Kin* (1984), *Family Viewing* (1987) and *Speaking Parts* (1989). His early work was dark, cerebral and frequently investigated family dysfunction and trauma. What has been fascinating about his career is the way he has embraced different styles and even cultures of film-making without losing touch with his original preoccupations. He has made literary adaptations (*The Sweet Hereafter*, 1997), Hollywood films (*Where the Truth Lies*, 2005), and has also explored his Armenian heritage (in *Calendar*, 1993, and *Ararat*, 2002). Egoyan has also directed theatre, opera and TV. He has worked as a teacher and has even opened his own cinema. He is an experimental film-maker who has made films that have piqued the curiosity of mainstream audiences.

Egoyan was born in 1960 in Cairo, Egypt. He was named Atom to mark the completion of Egypt's first nuclear reactor. In 1962, his family left Egypt for Canada. As a student at the University of Toronto, Egoyan became ever more aware of his Armenian background. Armenian history and, in particular, the Armenian genocide, are referred to explicitly in several of his films. As a teenager, his interest was as much in the theatre as in cinema. Egoyan is now based in Toronto, where he lives with his wife Arsinée Khanjian.

Atom Egoyan:

"For me, it's *Persona*. There are so many moments in that film but for me, it's that moment when the boy goes up with his hand and places it on the screen, the images of the two women, Liv Ullmann and Bibi Andersson, when they kind of merge, and the scene when Liv Ullmann is in the hospital bed watching the Vietnamese priest burn. There is this extraordinary monologue that Bibi Andersson has about her erotic experience. There is that ability to sustain that sexual energy just through narrative. There is the moment when Liv Ullmann is walking barefoot on the patio and Bibi Andersson sees the glass and doesn't warn her. All those scenes have real power. I come from a theatrical background and my first love was theatre but that was the film that made me realise that you could be involved in a screen drama with the same intensity that a theatrical experience could provide.

I saw the film in unusual circumstances. I was raised in a small city on the west coast of Canada, Victoria. It's a bilingual country. There was a French CBC station that used to show art films. As youngsters, we would watch it because they had racier movies on there. I was a teenager, thirteen or four- teen. That was the first time I saw it, in a French dubbed version. Then there was a campus theatre called Cine Centa. They had a retrospective of Bergman's films. I've actually kept the programme because it was a very form- ative experience. *Shame* was also very important for me. There is this extra- ordinary scene with Max von Sydow and Liv Ullmann having a picnic outside. It's a dialogue but it is entirely on Liv Ullmann's face. There is no reverse shot on to Max von Sydow. I just thought that was so unusual. I had never seen any- thing so strident. By not seeing his face, I had to imagine his face. It's a very, very delicate dialogue. They're talking about fidelity.

I still don't know – and I'll never ask him [Bergman] now whether it is a posi- tioning zoom. There is this very strong gesture the camera makes where it just moves very swiftly onto her face. It's just very powerful. It's a formal cine- matic gesture within a naturalist scene. That intervention and alchemy was really stirring and effective for me. I think another reason those images from *Persona* had such a strong effect on me was because they were painterly and I was very aware of painting through my parents (who were artists). At the beginning of the film, there is a

Shame (Ingmar
Bergman, 1968)

sequence with very overblown images – Christ's hands being nailed, the graphic combustion of the film and that kind of thing. The textural sense in watching that visual material presented was very inspiring because it was saying that film could be like painting. What I didn't realise is that it's almost an installation. When you have a film image that burns up on screen, that is implicating the viewers in a very specific way and making them self-conscious in a way that you wouldn't be in theatre. You're aware of how volatile or fragile that experience is. It's the same in the theatre because it's live – how an actor can forget a line or how something can just fall apart because it is real. That [with *Persona*] was the first time I realised that film had that same volatility, although it's far less likely to happen.

I have one treasured memory about Bergman. I was in Stockholm many years ago. Bergman had a small cinema where he used to watch films in Stockholm but most of his film-watching was on Faro. He would import films. The distributors in Stockholm used to lend him prints. I met this one academic who told me that Bergman loved an early film of mine, *Family Viewing*. I didn't believe that but he actually hunted down Bergman's request sheet.

I have in his own handwriting 'Family Viewing by Atom Egoyan'. He watched it. That was really emotional for me. Just before he died, he did an interview with a paper that was syndicated to Canada. He talked about young directors who were promising and he mentioned my name. I have that tacked on my wall at my office. I never met him. I'm very envious of my friend Olivier Assayas, who conducted some interviews with him.

The director I have had the closest contact with is Michelangelo Antonioni. I was shadowing one of his projects. It was a film that had been written by Rudi Wurlitzer. It was for Julianne Moore. I spent some time in LA with him. He was staying at John Malkovich's house. His films were also important to me, especially *La notte* and *Red Desert*. Having this opportunity to be with him was quite surreal. He was meeting the cream of all the young actresses in Hollywood at the time. I was seated behind him. None of them had been prepped as to the fact that he was completely paralysed – that he had had a stroke. In would walk these young women into Malkovich's house, fawn over Antonioni and say how much they loved *Blow-Up* and then realise at a certain point he wasn't responding – and then registering their dismay as they had to negotiate the fact that he was paralysed. That was quite perversely thrilling. I could communicate with him through his wife, Henrietta. When they were trying to tell me how easy he could be and how well it could work, they sent me a documentary of Wim Wenders working with him on *Beyond the Clouds*. Actually, if there was ever a repellent that could have been more effective, it was this documentary where you saw him trying to command what he wanted and Wim trying to accommodate it. It was kind of horrifying. I felt a tremendous debt to him but I think it would have been a very difficult working environment. In the end, the film never got made. It was an impossible project. He wanted to shoot it in the middle of LA. At the time, the middle of LA was incredibly dangerous, not like it is now. We used to do these location scoutings in the middle of gang-controlled areas. The film just never got financed. Even with my participation, I don't think they were able to get the insurance.

As a kid, I remember going to see films in Victoria. I went to see *The Sound of Music*. I remember going to see *The Sandpiper* with my grandmother before I knew English well. There was one horri-fying image where a person gets crushed to death by a piston in a steamship. I remember my grand-mother shielding me from watching this horrifying scene. Those were the early experiences. I wasn't one of those people consumed by the magic of cinema. It was really about theatre. Cinema came later on.

I had started making films on Super-8mm at high school. But it was mostly theatre I was interested in. Then I went to study at the University of Toronto. There was certainly a great film culture in Toronto when I moved there. I started writing reviews for the student paper. This festival of festivals had just begun. I wrote the first review of *Eraserhead* [by David Lynch] in a publication called *The Newspaper* at the University of Toronto. I was the film editor. *Eraserhead* was released in Canada in 1978 and I saw an early projection of it. I saw the press book. That was also formative. I had never seen anything quite like that. I was quite influenced by the early surrealist films like *Un chien anadalou*. I used to project those in Victoria. I started showing short films like Kenneth Anger, *Chien andalou* and early Polanski shorts. That sensibility was very exciting to me. Then I saw *Eraserhead* that was able to inherit and extend that tradition, espe-

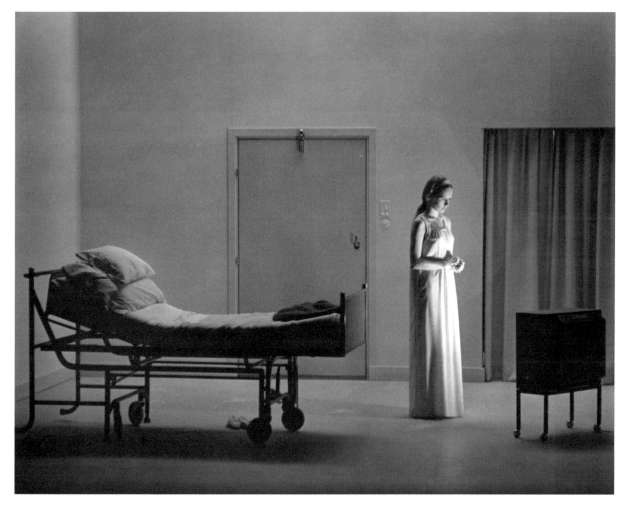

Persona

cially the sound design by Alan Splet. I remember that scene where the baby starts vomiting.

There were a number of films that I reviewed. I remember *Apocalypse Now* and *Cruising* and *Kramer vs. Kramer*. Then there was a whole slew of Fassbinder films. His films had a huge impact because of the theatricality. Like Bergman, he was coming from a theatre tradition. Films like *Fear Eats the Soul, Ali*, *Merchant of the Four Seasons* (that scene where he commits suicide by drinking himself to death), *Katzelmacher* – they were also very formative. In terms of epiphany, I'd have to say it's *Persona*. That just got me so excited.

And the biggest epiphany was a strange one. There was a series called the American Film Theatre devised by Eli Landau. The idea was that these films would travel to various cities that would never get the plays. After the projections, the prints would be destroyed. That was the theory. It would preserve the ephemeral nature of the experience. Of course, the films weren't destroyed. I was a huge Pinter fan. I went to see a production of Peter Hall's *The Homecoming*. That was very, very striking. There was this almost brutal approach to the editing. There were very strange compositions. It was photographed by David Watkins. I met him many years later and he explained how he shot it. I worked with Ian Holm on *The Sweet Hereafter* and I got stories from him as well. They were using very strong arc lights and then stopping down. They were using long lenses and they had incredible depth of field. The only way you could do that at the time was by bombarding light on the set. Apparently, it was unbearable to shoot. The actors were sweltering. But there were these very strange compositions as a result. I must have been in my teens when I saw it. It was just around that time when I was getting excited about theatre, especially the writings of Beckett and Pinter and the psychodramas of Strindberg. Between Bergman and Fassbinder and especially that production of *The Homecoming*, I saw there could be a marriage between those traditions.

I had been writing and directing plays from the age of thirteen or fourteen. They were derivative of a forgotten figure here called N. F. Simpson. Before The Goons and Monty Python, he was one of the formative figures in the English absurdist tradition. My parents were artists but I had one drama teacher who was so inspiring to me. His name was Colin Skinner, an Englishman transplanted to Victoria. He came from the panto tradition and he used to write plays at school. He used to join students in the process. I saw someone was who writing and directing theatre. I was in an early play of his called *Robot* and I played a figure called Atom. It was very exciting but there weren't really any film influences.

Years later, I had a very unusual relationship with a director who came to live in Victoria, George Cosmatos, who did *Rambo: First Blood Part II*. He was the first film director I met. There was a writer in Victoria called Michael Reid. He connected the two of us. I'll never forget this one Christmas, in 1993, when my son was very young. We took him by stroller to George Cosmatos's house. It was the weekend that *Tombstone* was released. I remember him fielding all these calls from Hollywood about grosses and then, at one point, he looked at me and said – how do you get your films invited to festivals? I just thought, my God, the grass is always greener. I thought – how do you get your film on 2,000 screens? That was what I really wanted to know. ❯❯

Barbet Schroeder

Voyage to Italy

(Roberto Rossellini, 1954)

Franco-Swiss director Barbet Schroeder, who was born in Iran in 1941, is one of the few film-makers associated with the French New Wave who has had a career as a Hollywood director. He is a producer as well as a director. His filmography is extraordinarily varied, encompassing revenge thrillers, biopics, political documentaries and high-minded arthouse films.

In the early 1960s, Schroeder was part of the *Cahiers du cinéma* set. He co-founded Les Films du Losange with Eric Rohmer. He appears as a very young man playing the lover torn between two women in Rohmer's delightful moral tale *The Baker of Monceau* (1963). He produced many of Rohmer's films (among them *Claire's Knee*, 1970, and *My Night with Maud*, 1969), as well as Jacques Rivette's *Celine and Julie Go Boating* (1974). Pink Floyd wrote the music for his first film as a director, *More* (1969), which was about heroin addiction.

Whether in his documentaries or in his fictional work, Schroeder is often drawn to charismatic, larger-than-life figures with a hint of madness about them. He directed a feature-length documentary on Ugandan dictator Idi Amin, *General Idi Amin Dada*, in 1974, as well as one on the French lawyer Jacques Vergès, whose client list included everybody from Carlos the Jackal to Klaus Barbie.

His best-known dramatic feature, *Reversal of Fortune* (1990), was about socialite Claus von Bulow, who was accused of murdering his wife. The film won Jeremy Irons an Oscar. Schroeder likes to cite his relatively little seen *Our Lady of the Assassins* (2000), about love and death in drug-ridden, gang-infested Colombia, as the film that gives him the most pride. However, many of his films have achieved a certain status. *Barfly* (1987), inspired by alcoholic American writer Charles Bukowski, boasted a famously eccentric performance from Mickey Rourke as the brawling, hard-drinking hero. *Single White Female* (1992) was galvanised by Jennifer Jason Leigh's performance as the vengeful psychopath and managed the trick of smuggling in elements from Bergman's *Persona* (1966) into an otherwise conventional Hollywood thriller.

At the same time as he was working with major American stars on genre films, Schroeder was also busy with his documentaries. He has appeared as an actor in French and American films, and recently was even ready to decamp to Japan to make the highly stylised geisha thriller, *Inju: The Beast in the Shadow* (2008). In his late sixties, his career choices continue to wrong-foot his followers.

Barbet Schroeder:

"I would choose a moment in *The Voyage to Italy* by Roberto Rossellini that is completely extraordinary, when Ingrid Bergman and George Sanders discover the couple that were making love but have died [in the Vesuvius eruption]. This is an extraordinary moment in which you connect completely with the emotion of the characters.

I saw the film in the Cinémathèque [in Paris] in the late 50s. It stimulated me to go and see all the other Rossellini movies and to watch again the ones I had already seen. I became very, very interested and influenced by Rossellini. I was already a cinephile and interested in his movies but that really multiplied my interest.

When I was a child in Bogota, I had a big problem with movies. The first time my parents took me to the movies, they had to take me out of the cinema theatre because I was crying so much ... it was *Bambi*! I had to be taken out. Then, after that, I didn't go to see movies because I had such a trauma the first time. I had been born in Iran, raised in South America and then came to France when I was eleven. My father was a geologist in all those places, except France because my parents were divorced by then.

I didn't go to the movies. Then, when I was in Paris at eleven, I didn't go to the movies immediately. I thought if I had to be taken out of that place [the cinema], maybe it was not a place for me. My mother took me to see some art movies. She was from a very artistic background. I remember the next movie I saw because my mother took me and said I had to see it. This was another shocker – *Night and Fog* by Alain Resnais, about the Nazi concentration camps. She said this is a must, an absolute must. That was my second movie after *Bambi*. She tried to explain to me what it was about but until you see it, you don't understand. I think I was about eleven and a half. That was in the Agriculture – a cinema where you had big leather seats, in the 9th *arrondissement* close to the Gare St Lazare. It was showing with something else. I don't even know if we stayed to see the other film.

Night and Fog made me think a lot and discover the century I was living in. It was very well done, a super-important movie. Then I discovered all the other movies of Alain Resnais and another short he did that was completely aesthetic about the making of plastic called *Le Chant du Styrène*. It was so beautifully made, the tracking shots, that I cried because of the beauty of the tracking shots.

Voyage to Italy

SCREEN EPIPHANIES

Night and Fog
(Alan Resnais,
1955)

At the time, there were some art-houses and I started seeing some films by Bergman. That was at the age of twelve.

I started going to the Cinémathèque Française every night and more and more. I ended up seeing two or three movies a day there and going to the café afterwards to discuss them. I was thirteen or fourteen and it went on till I was eighteen. I met all the people who became critics at the *Cahiers du cinéma* – Jean Eustache and Bertrand Tavernier, others who became film-makers but are not known. There was a whole group. We were the generation after the previous one [of Truffaut and Godard]. Henri Langlois [the co-founder of the Cinémathèque] would do homages. You could go and see the whole work of Ingmar Bergman from the very beginning to the very end or – more important – the whole work of Howard Hawks. It's an extraordinary thing. You suddenly see the relationship between all the films, you see the style, the approach, you see everything. It's the same for painting, when you see the whole work of a painter in one big exhibition, you have much more chance of understanding exactly that artist.

There were big fights between us. I was more extreme than some of the others in my championings of American cinema. It took me a long time to understand Renoir. We were less understanding of the New Wave. But that moment in *Voyage to Italy* is the one I would isolate if I want to choose an epiphany. **"**

Bertrand Tavernier

Fort Apache

(John Ford, 1948)

Born in Lyons in 1941, Tavernier is a large, enthusiastic, loquacious man with a fund of observations and anecdotes on any given subject always at his fingertips. His father was the writer and editor, René Tavernier, founder of a magazine called *Confluences* that published the work of Louis Aragon, Paul Eluard and others during the Occupation.

Tavernier has seen cinema from every side. As a teenager, he was one of those ardent cinephiles who used to haunt the Cinémathèque Française in Paris. He has written extensively about cinema (he even set up his own film magazine). Early in his career, he was a publicist, working with some of the leading New Wave directors and with Jean-Pierre Melville. Unlike most of his compatriots, he is enthusiastic about British cinema, especially the work of Powell and Pressburger and the best films produced at Ealing. Unafraid of swimming against the tide, early in his own directing career he worked closely with Jean Aurenche and Pierre Bost, the writers excoriated by François Truffaut as epitomising the 'Cinéma de Papa'.

Underlining his breadth of interest, Tavernier has directed films across all genres, including costume dramas (*The Judge and the Assassin*, 1976), film noir with an African slant (the Senegal-set Jim Thompson adaptation *Coup de torchon*, 1981), police procedurals (*L.627*, 1992), swashbucklers (*D'Artagnan's Daughter*, 1994), wartime films (*Laissez-passer*, 2002) and family dramas (*Daddy nostalgie*, 1990). If you had to think of a trademark Tavernier scene, it would be of gruff but marvellously expressive actor Philippe Noiret (who appeared in several of his films) at at table, chewing on a chicken leg. Tavernier relishes the conviviality and carnivalesque aspect of dinner table scenes – what they reveal about character and their potential for conspiracy and humour.

Bertrand Tavernier:

"I had thousands of epiphanies, and of different kinds. There were several which made me want to become a film director. I think when I was twelve or thirteen, I realised (maybe in a very superficial way) the person who was signing the film, 'directed by', was responsible for some ideas or images you could find in other films. That was very clear for me. The first person who made it clear that you could write with images the same way you could write with words, that you could find in films the same things you could find when you were reading the books of Jack London or Robert Louis Stevenson or Jules Verne, was John Ford. Within a few weeks of each other, I saw *Fort Apache* and *She Wore a Yellow Ribbon*. Definitely, there were similarities I saw in the images and themes, in the way people were filmed in wide shot. I was not so analytical but immediately, in the notebook I had, I drew in a few images of *Fort Apache* and I underlined 'A Film by John Ford'. That was the first moment ... the first three names I put in my notebook were Ford, Hathaway (for *Lives of a Bengal Lancer*) and William Wellman. It is when I decided at thirteen that I was going to be a film director.

I had seen *Fort Apache* in a small cinema in Avenue de la Grande Armée in a dubbed version made in 16mm. It was in a cinema that was one of my temples. It had two small theatres, most of the time playing American films. When I was in boarding school, practically every Sunday I was trying to go to that cinema. It is where I saw *Thieves' Highway*, it is where I saw a series called *Congo Bill*. I saw a big number of films there.

Why did I see these films? It was either because I looked at the title or I wanted to see a film with John Wayne or Gary Cooper. I liked the titles. I had already seen things written about John Ford – that he was a very important film-maker. Then I asked my godfather to take me to see *La Charge héroïque* [as *She Wore a Yellow Ribbon* was called in France]. That was another cinema, not far from Les Champs-Elysées. It must have been a re-release, the original version subtitled. It was the second shot that made me put John Ford on my map and decide that I would be a film director and not a lawyer – or anything else that my parents wished. Ford was responsible for this. And maybe *The Lives of a Bengal Lancer*.

With Ford, I liked those wide shots with the clouds. I liked those views of

Fort Apache

the rocky landscapes. That immediately impressed me. I remember noticing that the treatment of the Indian was not like in other films I was watching. They had a dignity in that film. I remember noticing the music. I never forgot it. And, as a young boy, I liked the attitude of Ford: the spirit of adventure, the way he dealt with emotions. There was something for me that was close to the text of Victor Hugo – a kind of epic feeling and at the same time an emotional feeling. I am talking about Hugo's poem *The Expiation*, which I used to know by heart, which my father used to read me when I was five or six, about the French retreat from Moscow. You had lines like 'ten thousand went to sleep, a hundred waked' or 'the wounded hid themselves in the bellies of dead horses'. For me, that was a kind of image I would not have been surprised to see in a Ford film. There is the fact that the guy playing the bugle is totally frozen. There was a sense of Kipling in John Ford too. I was seeing things that I had read in Kipling. I think Ford is close to Kipling. He took a certain notion of Kipling – the heroism that Kipling praised but also the dedication of the public servant. Without analysing, what I was finding in Hugo and maybe Kipling was a sense of values – a sense that the character

believed in what he was doing. It was the same feeling I had when I read what Jack London was describing in *White Fang* or that Jules Verne was writing about in *Captain Nemo*.

The photography in *She Wore a Yellow Ribbon* seemed to me very beautiful, with red sunlight and red sunsets. The melancholy of the film escaped me. The fact that Wayne is talking to his dead wife escaped me. I was attracted by other things – for example, the operation during the storm.

A lot of the time, I went to the cinema alone. I remember taking my grandmother to some terrible cinemas in Lyon because I wanted to see *Gunga Din*. She was very frightened of the cinema where I was taking her. For her, it was full of Arabs. My father was always taking me to see films with subtitles. I remember seeing *Distant Drums* by Raoul Walsh and loving it. But most of the time I was alone and I was always going to cinemas which were playing very old films, dubbed most of the time. I didn't have a lot of money. I saw *The Wake of the Red Witch*, which I loved, three times in a row. Most of the films I saw in this period I still like very much.

Later on, I had a new shock in the cinema when I saw for the first time *La Grande Illusion*. This was four or five

Bob le flambeur
(Jean-Pierre
Melville, 1956)

years afterward. I must have been about seventeen. Suddenly, I felt I was seeing something else. The heroism was treated in a totally different way. I felt that compared to a lot of films I was seeing, it was more mature. It was more daring. There was a complexity of feeling. My father was a great help. He could help me understand the period. He was telling me about the historical context of some of those films. That was very rewarding. I remember staying twice. That happened to me three times – also with *Shadow of a Doubt* and *Kiss Me Deadly*. They were the three films I saw twice in a row. In some cases, I came back the next day. I found a great

humanism in Aldrich, even if it takes place in the opposite way [to Renoir]. I think it is close to Renoir. He is still one of my favourite directors. He expressed it in a violent way but there is a belief in Aldrich, a need for humanism.

Then I saw *Les Enfants du paradis*. Then, I had a series of discoveries – for example, the first time I saw *Singin' in the Rain*. There have been a lot of films I have found provocative. But I remember receiving an immediate shock at the photography and use of light in Melville's *Bob le flambeur*. It seemed very, very new – the work of the cinematographer Henri Decae. That was something I hadn't seen before. **”**

Mike Newell

La Grande Illusion

(Jean Renoir, 1937)

It used to be said of Mike Newell, Michael Apted and Stephen Frears that they 'left no footsteps behind them'. This was both a barb and a compliment. To their detractors, these three English directors, all close contemporaries, had no clear personal signature. There were no overriding ideas or themes in their work. They could work on TV dramas and soap operas, on British contemporary movies or on costume dramas, or even on documentaries, without any noticeable discomfiture. A more generous, fairer assessment is that these three directors were supremely versatile. Oxbridge-educated, humanistic in outlook, they had been taught their profession in television during a golden period for small-screen drama. As a result, they were able to turn their hands to almost anything.

Born in St Albans in 1942, Newell directed *Four Weddings and a Funeral* (1994), one of the most successful British films of the 1990s. This was the romantic comedy that made Hugh Grant into an international star and seemed to signal the arrival of PolyGram as a major international player. Critics weren't especially kind about a movie that seemed to many mainstream and even saccharine. They didn't seem to notice the pacing, the structure, the attention to performance that are always hallmarks of Newell's films. His ability had first really become evident with *Dance with a Stranger* (1985), a brilliantly observed, moving and ultimately very grim drama about Ruth Ellis, the last woman to be hanged in Britain. The film exposed the sexual and social hypocrisy prevalent in 1950s Britain. From these relatively intimate and small-scale beginnings, Newell has gone on to make some very big movies indeed – the brilliant mobster drama *Donnie Brasco* (1997), an instalment of the Harry Potter franchise and, most recently, *Prince of Persia: The Sands of Time* (2010), for Jerry Bruckheimer.

Mike Newell:

"I have a very particular 'epiphany'. It's *La Grande Illusion*.

My dad, who I adored, was very interested in amateur theatricals. He never did theatre professionally. He was of the generation of the Depression when to have a job at all was a very wonderful thing. He was a quantity surveyor. He worked out how many million nails it would take to build an office block. He wasn't going to piss about with professional theatre but he did absolutely love the theatre and was mixed up in all sorts of amateur theatricals. He read colossally. And he had an equal devotion to France and anything French. He was tremendously excited by French movies. They had been new and fresh to him when he was in his early twenties, in the 30s.

My father took me when I was fifteen or sixteen to the Academy on Oxford Street – the old Academy, the one with the flock wallpaper in the main house. We went to a performance of *La Grande Illusion*. With it, I saw a cartoon called *The Little Island*. I can't remember who made it but it was some famous and modish cartoon-maker of the time. I also saw a newsreel in which the very first Aldermaston march was featured. There was this extraordinary shot of a man with a sandwich board around his neck walking along some terribly rainy, Scottish Highland road on his way to Aldermaston. All three of these things made an enormous impression on me but the main movie [*La Grande Illusion*] hit a very particular kind of nerve. I've always remembered it in great detail and it set all sorts of things going in me. I would not have gone down the road I did without that, I think. It was very clear to me and very precise. It wasn't the anti-war message. I was generally aware of that because I was born during the Second World War and so all my uncles had gone through the war. Nobody wanted to talk about it and nobody ever really did talk about it. I don't think they suffered in any great way. They were in Burma mostly. The war that I had focused on and was beginning to be much more aware of was the First War. It was the great literary war. I was beginning to be aware of the collision between Victorian sensibility and a modern factory method of [destruction]. I was aware of the First World War having been some colossal upheaval which wasn't just a matter of a great many people being killed in all sorts of dreadful ways. It was bigger than that.

There are some scenes in *La Grande Illusion* that I particularly remember.

One was the scene between the two aristocrats – the French aristocrat Captain de Boëldieu [played by Pierre Fresnay] and the German aristocrat Captain von Rauffenstein [Erich von Stroheim], who is wearing the neck brace. They were from the same class. Their shared assumptions and lives and friends brought them together. They all knew the same people. They talk about the same horse race, the Liverpool Cup. They talk in three languages. They talk in French, they talk in German and they talk in English and they swap, absolutely smoothly, from one to the other. You see that class for them is way beyond national conflicts. You also see that they are dying – that their type is not going to survive. Whereas Lieutenant Marechal, the character played by Jean Gabin, is going to survive because he is full of a vigour that they don't quite have.

I couldn't have possibly rationalised the film like that at the time I saw it [as a teenager] but it was very exciting to see that was clearly what was going on. I had never come across a film in which apparently inconsequential dialogue like that had such a kind of ringing energy and juice in it. I didn't know why it was. I just gathered there was juice there. The neck brace that Von Stroheim

is in, the way that you have two apparent enemies who are not enemies at all. All those extraordinary opposites was something that I remembered very clearly and do to this day.

No, I wasn't aware that Renoir had directed it – but I sure as hell became so. I don't think I said I will try to be a film director from that moment on. But what I did think was that this was better than most things I had seen.

When I was a little younger, I had seen *Bad Day at Black Rock*. I remember going to that on my tenth birthday. My mother just got sick of us. She said it is two shillings each. Go and get lost for an afternoon. Somehow or another, I don't know how we did it, we got in to see *Bad Day at Black Rock* and then we came back and we acted it out in the field next to the house. Of course, what everybody wanted to do was to be the people who bumped Spencer Tracy, the one-armed cop, off the road in the jeep in that great sequence. They were the bad guys in this little town in the desert who tried to drive him off the road. We all wanted to do that. Nobody wanted to be Spencer Tracy. Everybody wanted to be the people who knocked him off the road.

I never thought about film directing at all. I was potty about the theatre because my father and mother were

La Grande Illusion

potty about the theatre. They used to take me all the time and do their own amateur productions. They were very state-of-the-art theatre literate. I found my father's copy of *Waiting for Godot* the other night. It was a first edition. So he was reading the play within two or three months of it having been translated into English. I read a lot. I read my father's bookshelves. He had all these plays. I was reading those when I was ten. Not to make myself anything extraordinary – they were just around and when you were bored you took a book out. The only thing that was going was a play – so I began to read dialogue much more easily than I read any other form. He was pretty much up with the game. I used to see a lot of plays – a lot of good plays – as well. Eugene O'Neill, modern Irish writers, Ibsen. All sorts of stuff. They [my parents] didn't do big West End hits. They wanted to do good stuff. I was actually mixed up in it. That was where I thought I was going to go. I didn't. I went into television. Then, as soon as I saw there was a way of adjusting the proscenium arch with the choice of lenses, then I got pretty interested. Then I began to think about the trade of it. But the impact of it [cinema] was a long time before that and was very clear to me.

The influence [of Renoir] was through osmosis. You took these things in through the soles of your feet and then you started to work in this great new populist medium, TV. In *La Règle du jeu*, Renoir said 'chacun a ses raisons' ['everyone has his reasons']. I thought that was the most glorious basis for stories. It means you can deal with everything. You can deal with a murderer and if you see his reasons and if you understand what his reasons are, that is not a perverse thing to do. It is not a perverse thing to study extremes. Those French guys pre-New Wave did that all the time.

It wasn't that *La Grande Illusion* led me on to *La Règle du jeu*. I didn't go hunting Renoir. I think that what happened to me was that I instinctively started to tabulate the stuff I got really excited about. I was simply omnivorous. I would take what I could get. If you asked me what are the movies I saw, I saw *Bad Day at Black Rock*, *The Nutty Professor*, *Julius Caesar* – a mile of Westerns of all kinds of quality. We didn't have TV until quite late. So I used to go either to the theatre or to movies. It was a good day when there was an American movie and it wasn't quite such a good day when there was a British movie. But there were things like *Genevieve* and *The Dam*

Busters as well as all the American stuff. It was only later, when I started to be an undergraduate, that I saw there was a kind of literature there – that movies were a literature.

What I pursued in my work was emotional and psychological realism. Television was full of that stuff at that point. It was a glorious time in TV and a rotten time in the movies. We were lucky enough to be in TV. If you look at the first six episodes of *Coronation Street*, they have the force of a great truth. If you look at the first six episodes of *Z Cars*, they have the force of truth to them. There was this discovery going on about the world that we lived in which was that everybody lived in it and that stories belonged to everybody. Everybody had them and everybody had a right to have them told. We were in the north of England. Not one of my friends had been further north than Barnet. All of a sudden, we were in this very strong Lancashire culture which was great – very exciting – but it had to be learned. You'd say something somebody didn't like and they'd say I hope your rabbit ups and dies. You'd say, what! You had to relearn the language. Then, of course, at the same time, you were going through immense frustration because you couldn't tell the stories that you could see were there in a sufficiently subtle way.

Michael Apted, Steve Frears and me were all in the same year at Cambridge. We all kind of knew one another. Apted and I were colossal best friends for years and years. We were 'GPs' – general purpose vehicles. That was fantastic fun. That's where all the energy was. **"**

Ken Loach

The Fireman's Ball

(Milos Forman, 1967)

Ken Loach on the
set of *Kes* (1969)

Ken Loach is among the most revered British film-makers of his generation. Other directors whose work is very different from his and who don't share his politics nonetheless frequently cite him as their key formative influence. Loach's career divides into two halves. In 1966, he made the ground-breaking *Cathy Come Home*, a TV drama shot in documentary style that provoked a huge public debate about homelessness. Somehow, Loach had managed to help set the news agenda with a piece of fiction. A reported 12 million people watched *Cathy Come Home*.

Loach liked to think locally and to use actors (often non-professionals) who were close to the characters they were portraying. This was certainly the case in his 1969 masterpiece *Kes*, about a teenage boy who adopts and trains a kestrel hawk. Billy Casper is lively, rebellious and funny but he lives on a rough housing estate and seems destined to end up working in the mines. As in all of Loach's best films, the personal and the political are intertwined. Lyricism and agitprop sit side by side. The director has a talent for characterisation, and it was surely his ability to portray the yearnings and contradictions of his protagonists that so impressed the Polish director Krzysztof Kieślowski, who became a fervent admirer. At the same time, Loach never retreats into an abstract realm or shows his protagonists in isolation from the society in which they live. He is always conscious of class, of oppression.

Loach's goal is always to capture what he calls 'authenticity of experience'. His reputation as a polemicist who shoots in his own gritty, realist style is so ingrained that critics are sometimes oblivious to the humour in his movies and to the delicate way in which he treats relationships. Whether it's the celebrated football scene in *Kes*, the comic set-pieces involving postmen wearing Eric Cantona masks in *Looking for Eric* (2009), the scene of Ricky Tomlinson trying to hunt a sheep in *Raining Stones* (1993) or Peter Mullan taking on the world in *My Name Is Joe* (1998), Loach's films have a free-wheeling vitality about them. He doesn't just chronicle economic and social deprivation; Loach also celebrates the richness and defiance in Britain's working-class culture.

In the Thatcher years of the 1980s, Loach endured a relatively barren period. He re-emerged with *Hidden Agenda* (1990), a drama set against the backcloth of the shoot-to-kill policy in Northern Ireland. Since then, he has found it easier to secure funding for his features, which have shown to huge acclaim at international festivals.

Ken Loach:

" Epiphanies? Not really. The biggest thing for me was when I saw Joan Littlewood's work – those plays like *Fings Ain't Wot They Used t'Be* and *Oh! What a Lovely War* that she did at Stratford East. They were as significant as anything else to me because there was a real celebration of working-class life, which is one of the things that has propelled me and other writers I've worked with. I learned a lot from stills photographers as well. Films not so much, because I came into the theatre and then I went from the theatre to television. The influence in the beginning was more from the documentaries, from *World in Action*.

When I was smaller, I lived quite near Stratford-upon-Avon. I used to cycle over there to see plays rather than go to the cinema. I was much more orientated toward the theatre.

The films that had the biggest impact on me were the Czech films by Milos Forman and Jiri Menzel – particularly Forman's films *Loves of a Blonde* and *The Fireman's Ball*. It was the unmelodramatic way they just observed people with some sense of shared humanity. I liked the technical aspect – the framing, the lighting and the lenses they used, the stillness of it, the quiet observation. What I remember are the long lenses. Maybe there would be a little compression of the image. They seemed to avoid the wide-angle lenses, which I didn't like anyway. The scene in the dance hall in *Loves of a Blonde* sticks with me. It was very simple, humorous and thoughtful. And when the girl goes back to the boy's parents, that scene is also beautifully observed.

We were very aware of the Prague Spring. We went to Karlovy Vary [a film festival in Czechoslovakia] just before the Soviet tanks came in and just afterwards. We heard the news of the Soviet invasion just when we were shooting *Kes*. Chris Menges had worked with Miroslaw Ondrícek, the cameraman who had worked on some of the Czech films, on *If …..* .

They [the Czech directors] confirmed what I was edging towards anyway but I think theatre and stills photography were more significant for me. Obviously, Cartier-Bresson had an influence. There were also the older photographers – a photographer called Frank Sutcliffe. I remember a book called *The Family of Man*. There were very dramatic, touching and authentic pictures. Bill Brandt, I remember his pictures from the 30s. It was just observation, finding drama in the everyday. He created very strong images of people at work.

The Fireman's Ball

It sounds a little mean but the British New Wave wasn't as influential. Obviously, they were closer to home. The group I was with obviously realised it was important those films were made but we saw them as a spur to try to take the next step. A number of films were made in the north of England over a short number of years and then they all went away. You felt there was an element of fashion about it rather than a long commitment. Actors would come in who just did the accent. We felt there was another step to be taken there. We were more critical because we were in the same business. In some of those British films, there was a theatricality about them – the performances and the way they were lit. The Czech films just came a few years later and seemed to transcend that and to be more cinematic. I saw them at the Academy – the much missed Academy. I've seen them again but often the memory is better. If you see them at a certain age, you'll see them differently from when you're a hardened old crow.

Epiphany? That's a bit heavy-breathing for me. There are just things that you note and you remember. I think 'epiphanies' is a bit melodramatic. **"**

Michael Apted

Wild Strawberries

(Ingmar Bergman, 1957)

Michael Apted is something of a chameleon of the film world: the 65-year-old director who changes colours with remarkable facility. On the one hand, he is a member of the Hollywood establishment – a Brit who has blossomed in the studio system. Apted is currently President of the Directors Guild. On the other, he is also one of that generation of British directors who went to Oxbridge, trained at the BBC or Granada and can seemingly turn their hands to anything.Apted's filmography runs the gamut from James Bond to episodes of *Coronation Street* – and he is not ashamed of it: 'Soderbergh has a wonderful line about that: there are two sorts of directors – people who have a style and find material to fit that style and directors who find material and find a way to fit the material … you can look at three or four of my films and you can't believe that they were made by the same person.'

Apted points to two key formative moments in his life. One was when he was eight years old and was taken by his father to see West Ham play football for the first time ('We beat Bury 4–0'). He has been supporting West Ham for over fifty years, and has been a season ticket-holder at Upton Park for twenty years. Not many other West Ham season ticket-holders live in Los Angeles ('It makes Saturdays very stressful, I tell you'). When he is in the UK, he'll seldom miss a home game, and during his time in LA, he'll watch the games on satellite TV. 'If it's a Saturday game, you go down at 7 in the morning. They serve an English breakfast and beer. If it's a big game, there are tons of people there, all with their stuff on, shouting and roaring. You can see a lot of games.' The other formative experience, as detailed below, was seeing *Wild Strawberries*.

Apted read law at Cambridge University, where his fellow students included comedian John Cleese, theatre director Trevor Nunn, future England cricket captain Mike Brearley, Mike Newell (who is godfather to his oldest son) and Stephen Frears. In 1963, he was taken on by Granada Television, where he worked as a researcher on the first of the *Seven Up* documentaries in 1964 and directed episodes of Britain's favourite soap opera, *Coronation Street*, another key career moment. 'Seeing Violet Carson and Pat Phoenix [legendary *Coronation Street* stars of the time] storming out of the rehearsal rooms in 1966 in Manchester was wonderful training for whatever lies ahead,' Apted remarks, promptly embarking on a seemingly unrelated digression about 'tracking those bloody gorillas around day after day for eight weeks' on *Gorillas in the Mist* (1988).

At Granada, Apted directed documentaries, news and entertainment programmes, and began to work with writers like Colin Welland, Arthur Hopcraft and Jack Rosenthal on television films. He went freelance in 1970 (on the basis that 'there's no such thing as a free lunch', he still refuses to sign long-term contracts with anybody) and directed his first feature, *Triple Echo*, with Glenda Jackson and Oliver Reed, two years later.

Apted realised that in most of the features he'd made, including *Stardust* (1974, for which actor Larry Hagman was foisted on him by Columbia the day shooting began), all the key decisions were taken by the American financiers. 'I thought this is crazy. I should go to where these decisions are made. I should go to the centre of what is driving the film industry, which is Hollywood. Anyway, I was tired of England, tired of the struggle to make films, disillusioned with the insularity. This was the England of Douglas-Home, Edward Heath, with its anti-European aspect of that and its class system, which in my *Seven Up* films I'd made a kind of analysis of.'

His initial experiences in Hollywood weren't happy ones. He was hired by producer Ray Stark to make a *Fame*-like story about kids in a New York artistic academy. He was all set to shoot the film when Stark mentioned, in passing, that the leading roles had been offered to Tatum O'Neal and David Cassidy. This was more than Apted could stomach. He walked off the production. By chance, his agent had, by then, put him up to direct *Coalminer's Daughter* (1980), about the life of country singer Loretta Lynn. Universal didn't have high hopes for the film, and intended to spend as little money as possible on production and to try to make a profit on the soundtrack album. Apted and his stars, Sissy Spacek and Tommy Lee Jones, were left to their own devices. They came up with a minor classic, a heart-warming but gritty backwoods yarn that received a hatful of Oscar nominations. 'I was in Los Angeles, extricating myself from Ray Stark … That was one of the big breaks of my life. I was preparing to go back to England, resigned to a life at the BBC or Granada and suddenly this happened.'

Coalminer's Daughter was the perfect calling card for Apted in the US. Like his fellow Brit Alan Parker, he thrived in Hollywood. In contrast, his old friend David Puttnam, who briefly became studio boss at Columbia, did not. 'He [Puttnam] couldn't ever stomach the rules of Hollywood,' Apted reflects. 'Well, if you can't stomach it, don't do it. That was the basic fundamental conflict in his life which made him seriously ill. He couldn't deal with Mike Ovitz and the agents. He couldn't deal with movie stars. He liked controlling what he did, but he couldn't stomach the Hollywood system. You can try and move it around and get it to serve you, which is what I try to do, but you're only moving it a millimetre. He tried to take it head-on. It can't be done. It was awful for him. The Columbia experience wrecked his dream of films. Film became contaminated for him from that moment on.'

Thankfully, Apted's own experience in Hollywood has been much more positive. Today, he remains as prolific as ever, still directing big-budget movies (the James Bond yarn *The World Is Not Enough*, 1999, and an instalment of the Narnia franchise, forthcoming) as well as exploring documentaries and dramas.

Michael Apted:

" There was a film that showed me movies could be more than Saturday-night entertainment. I saw it by chance because I used to go to school at the City of London School, which was by Blackfriars Bridge. That gave me access to the West End and to cinemas. I don't quite remember how I got there, but when I was sixteen, I found myself at the old Academy on Oxford Street. *Wild Strawberries* was on. I saw it and it was a total epiphany. I realised that a film could carry serious ideas. Up till then, movies to me had been about following girls and having popcorn entertainment. This, in a sense, changed my whole life. I don't know whether the film itself was something I would consider to be a powerful influence on the sort of work I ended up doing, but it was a certainly a life-changing experience being in that cinema, watching that movie.

As a teenager, I was extremely interested in the theatre; very interested in books; interested in the world of literary ideals. I lived in Ilford. My mother had got me interested in the entertainment business in terms of seeing seaside shows when we went on holiday and we listened to the radio. My mother had an interest in popular culture – in radio

and in the music hall. But my real culture was fashioned by being at the City of London School, where there was tremendous interest in the theatre. They did very elaborate and sophisticated school plays. We used to make field trips to West End theatres and stuff like that. I was culturally pretty sophisticated for a sixteen-year-old because of the access I had.

So one afternoon, I went on my own after school to see *Wild Strawberries* and that was my discovery of the magic element of the cinema. The idea seemed smart and interesting. The fact that it was about an old man going back into his own life wasn't a problem. I wasn't looking for the 50s version of *Star Wars*. I had had a serious literary upbringing and so I could absorb easily a serious literary film. In a sense, it was about expanding my literary and theatrical interests into movies. It wasn't a kind of movie epiphany. It wasn't like seeing a John Ford film and saying, oh, my God – here's a motion picture! I saw it more as being about ideas – literary ideas. I've tried to wean myself off that bit. I now look at stuff less as literary work and more as movie work and an art unto itself. Definitely, my interest is literary. Bergman's films are very literary. They're very visual but they're about

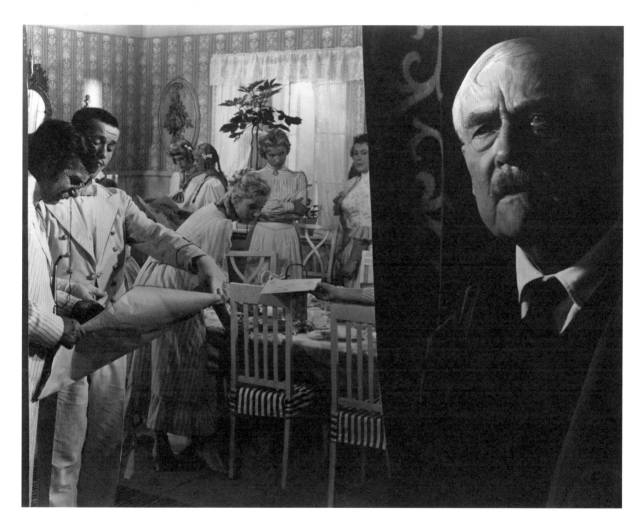

Wild Strawberries

coherent relationships. People talk a lot in Bergman films. It seemed a natural progression from the theatre and books into movies, via that. I began to investigate more of Bergman – I remember *The Seventh Seal* vividly, *The Virgin Spring* and the more psychological ones that followed, but *Wild Strawberries* was the key to the door. I think it was the literary power of Bergman that transfixed me. I could see that film was a poetic and visual medium but my access to it was through my literary instincts. I didn't direct anything until I went to Cambridge, but once I saw that movie and absorbed it, I really wanted to be a movie director.

My whole history of moviegoing was really after *Wild Strawberries*. I became totally enamoured of European cinema when I was at Cambridge University and afterwards when I joined Granada. Emotionally, I was more interested in the Italian neo-realists. I liked the social awareness. That appealed to me because I was quite political. It wasn't a strident politics but a more humanitarian politics which I got from my mother. I moved from Bergman to the neo-realists and from the neo-realists to Visconti. Then I became disillusioned with it as I began to work in television and had to earn a living doing it and had

to see my work as a livelihood. I couldn't just look at film as an academic or aesthetic pleasure. It was going to be the way that I was making a living. So I became disillusioned with European cinema. I felt it was elitist and preaching to the choir and not concerned with the practicalities of putting bums on seats. The great European cineastes became for me too esoteric, too disassociated from the world as I understood it.

I became enamoured with American cinema of the 70s, having never really been much interested in American cinema before that. I had never been much interested in Ford or Hawks or Preston Sturges or Billy Wilder, all of whom I discovered subsequently. My aesthetics were developed through European cinema and then my career orientation, my goals, were developed by that great period of America encompassing everything from *Dog Day Afternoon* to *Deliverance* to *Midnight Cowboy* to *The Godfather*. There were an endless group of entertaining and intelligent films that were in the marketplace and attempted to reach a larger audience. In that cinema, I found my ultimate synthesis – the aesthetic and the commercial. European cinema let me down. While it was long on aesthetics, it was pretty short on commercial viability. If I was going to earn a living making films, I realised I had better pay attention to how you make a living – how you sustain yourself and make a body of work. If I was to pick three films that really influenced me, it would be *Rocco [and His Brothers]*, *Nashville* and *Some Like It Hot*.

If I was to have a life-changing film, it would have to be something like *Rocco and His Brothers*, which introduced me to Italian neo-realism. Visconti was all over the place. There was a mixture of theatricality and realism that impacted on me.

Breathless was a great moment for me too, a technological epiphany – it was just the vitality, freedom, looseness of the whole thing that was devastating to me.

The realism of cinema and its worldliness rather than the slightly artificial world of the theatre appealed to me. *Wild Strawberries* was the key that unlocked the door [to cinema]. It was a door that could deal with literary and political themes. It wasn't really much of a love affair, me and Bergman. I fell in love with films and he was the conduit … but he wasn't one of my lovers! ⟩⟩

Jeremy Thomas

Badlands

(Terrence Malick, 1973)

Jeremy Thomas has been called a 'veteran producer' since he was in his late thirties. By then, he had already won a Best Picture Oscar for producing Bernardo Bertolucci's *The Last Emperor* (1987). Although his tastes and sensibility are very different to those of the old Ealing boss Michael Balcon, he is as close as contemporary British cinema comes to a producer with such a profile and impact.

Thomas knows the film business inside out. Given his family background, it could hardly be otherwise. His father, Ralph Thomas (director of the *Doctor* films), gave him a wind-up Bolex camera when he was thirteen. His uncle Gerald (later to direct all the *Carry On* films) taught him editing. His relative Victor Saville, a leading British producer and director in the 1930s, was another mentor.

When he left public school, he took a job in a film lab, which was the only way to get his union card. He worked in the cutting rooms and as a loader ('hence my familiarity with handling film in a tactile way'). On set, he's a jack of all trades. When Bertolucci started shooting *The Last Emperor*, the editor failed to arrive on time. Predictably, it was Thomas who cut the rushes together.

He is sure-footed when dealing with film-makers, agents and financiers, but lobbying government ministers is a different matter. In his years as Chairman of the British Film Institute, Thomas often had to deal with secretaries of state who had no interest in cinema. He claims that working with bureaucrats and Whitehall mandarins was infinitely more taxing than trying to raise millions of dollars for, say, a Bertolucci film.

The Brits have never known quite what to make of Thomas's internationalism. Critics like the late Alexander Walker of the *Evening Standard* or Christopher Tookey were sometimes appalled by his forays into arthouse cinema, while David Cronenberg's J. G. Ballard adaptation *Crash* (1996) and Nic Roeg's *Bad Timing* (1980), both Thomas productions, rubbed more conventional reviewers up the wrong way. His frequent collaborator Bertolucci once famously called him 'a hustler in the fur of a teddy bear' (he meant it as a compliment). Thomas's influence remains as profound today as it has for the last three decades. He is British cinema's one true internationalist. At a time when there has been pressure for British film-makers to look inward, he has never taken the parochial or nationalist point of view. Nor has he ever clung to the safe or familiar.

Jeremy Thomas:

"Cinema? I am pretty unusual because thankfully I was born in it – right into the cooking pot of film. My father had a 16mm projector. He got very new films on 16mm. I can remember changing the spools and snapping the reels at our house. My dad used to bring home these boxes. They were to go on this Bell and Howell projector. We projected on this screen at our house. Most weekends, we'd have a movie. We would be seeing the latest films of the time. We were also taken often to London to see movies. *South Pacific* I remember going to – and *The Horse Soldiers*, which I saw in Leicester Square. I remember *How the West Was Won* and going to Cinerama – big spectacular films. And the British comedies – the Ealing comedies. I'd go to Leicester Square or the Empire or the Odeon, Leicester Square, or one of the cinema palaces: the impact was frightening, it was so powerful – bloodshed, battle, John Wayne. The war was not so distant. It was an era of heroism and war was very strong. There were films like *The Dam Busters*, Googie Withers films, *Reach for the Sky*, *Battle of the River Plate* and *Sink the Bismark*. They always had Anthony Quayle or Anthony Quinn in them. They melded into one but they were powerful. Those seemed strong to me. My dad had made one war film, *Above Us the Waves*. I was a young boy reading comics like *The Eagle*. The heroics were still there. War, heroism and heroic nature were much reflected on in the films of the time.

I was in the same form at school as Jack Hawkins's son, Nick Hawkins. And John Mills's son, Jonathan Mills. Both Hawkins and Mills had worked with my dad, and Kenneth More had been in the house. I remember going to see *A Night to Remember* [about the *Titanic*] being made. I went to the backlot. I saw all these people climbing down this boat that was tipped up in the backlot. To a small boy, this boat was just gigantic. The sinking was being shot in the backlot. That was very powerful. When I saw the movie, I put two and two together. Later, I began making early teenage visits to the Curzon cinema, the NFT and the repertory cinemas to see films like *Belle de jour* or *My Sister My Love* or *I Am a Curious Yellow*.

The Paris Pullman, the Academy, the Electric – there was a fantastic set of repertory cinemas in London, showing a huge variety of films. It was a hip thing to be in the know about world cinema. Still, as a viewer, I remember seeing *Cathy Come Home* on telly. That was an incredibly strong thing. I saw the films on Kubrick and Nic Roeg. *Performance* was an incredible experience for me. And, of course, *2001* got me. It was an amazing thing being in the front row of the cinema, watching the bone. Every time a Kubrick film came out, I was there, the first day, queuing to go. I don't know if it's like that now. Occasionally, you get it still. You go and see an amazing film with other people in the Palais [at Cannes] or in a great screening room.

I grew very interested in cinema. I was a very bad student. I was dreaming a lot but I was not a good student. I had been working with a friend making a little film. I was at boarding school but in the holidays, I'd just want to go to the studios. It was the most exciting thing. It was impossible not to be attracted to going into the movie business after seeing what was at that time, to a child, an incredibly glamorous occupation. That technical toy set of film-making that was the studio system. That can't be found today because it's not there. You can't go down to Pinewood and find it full of movie stars and five films being made, the place full of work, people walking around in strange costumes. Of course, I've romanticised it in my mind. I was born in 1949. I can remember a bit of rationing.

When I left school, I went to work in the laboratories. Then I ended up working for Ken Loach for many years. And I ended up working with Karel Reisz as well. They were admired film-makers for me. Jack Clayton I admired. There were amazing film-makers. There are not film-makers like that making films now because there is not the need for them. There was no television and no video games. There was a need domestically to create this amount of material. They had to have films coming out all the time for the domestic market about domestic themes with domestic actors in them, and all these fantastic directors were making films. I can understand people sitting looking at the Rank films and the other films and feeling they were excluded by their style, politics and need to be different.

There is a moment at the beginning when every young man wants to cut loose from home. I cut loose, but I cut loose with people who were incredibly stimulating to be with – Tony Garnett and Ken Loach, Perry Henzell [*The Harder They Come*] and others. It was very exciting to be working as an assistant editor in an industry with full employment where you can go from place to place to get a job. You could go from film to film and choose, in a way, what area of culture you were moving toward and try to work there. I came into contact with Sandy Lieberson and David Puttnam and got a job editing film. All that time, I was still seeing films.

I still see films. I am a bit lazy about it now but the films I want to see the most, I will try to see in the cinema. I was still a student when I saw Bertolucci's first films. Bernardo started directing films very young. I can remember seeing *The Conformist*. That was strong and when the opportunity came to work with Bernardo, he was somebody I admired incredibly – an inspiring film-maker. I love it when you can get a film which is full of ideas – ideas, people talking about things that are arresting and stimulating. Where has the dialogue gone in films? Where have the ideas gone? I went to an event with Harold Pinter and David Hare talking. They were saying how their screen work was very important – in some cases as important as their stage work. The dialogue is so incredible in their films. The dialogue from *The Pumpkin Eater* and *Accident* was so fantastic.

When I saw *Badlands*, I was very moved by it – very moved by the size of it and the sense of it coming at you, the sensibility of the director, the whole feeling of the film, the freshness of it. How wonderful it was to see that film. Now, whenever you turn the television on, you see *Badlands*, but that was an important film to me. I didn't know anything about Terrence Malick at the time. The Martin Sheen character was a wonderful character – a completely split personality, socially very, very strange. It was a tour de force from Sheen in the vein of James Dean. Sissy Spacek was translucent and beautiful as the young girl. Warren Oates played the dad. How could you do better with an American indie movie? I could identify with the scale of it as an aspiring film-maker. When you think of a film by Stanley Kubrick at the time, how could you aspire to that? It was impossible even to think about making a film like *2001* or *Dr. Strangelove*. They were awesome things, just too big. How can you get there? How can you possibly promote something that is that big? *Badlands* was a really strong film and I could see how I could be involved with a film like that. Then, of course, the aspiration changes and you want to make the biggest films. But *Badlands* came at that strong moment for American independent films when there were the Bob Rafelson films, *King of Marvin Gardens* and *Five Easy Pieces*. There was *Easy Rider*.

Badlands

Those American indie movies in the early 70s, the Hal Ashby films, those groups of people – they were also very strong and influential to me. I was really drawn to independent films rather than thinking my career path was going to be set in a more commercialised area. I had a flirtation with that but it came back to the roots of what I liked as a young person. When you're pre-teen, early teen, you haven't really made your mind up. It is very rare to find a child or a young person who can be critical and intellectualise why they like or don't like something. Later, you start analysing what you like and what you don't like. It's late teens I suppose – in late, late teens, you start focusing your attention more on likes and dislikes.

I have incredible affection and even love for the films that my father and uncle made with the *Carry Ons* and *Doctors*. But I didn't want to make films like that. As a reaction, I wanted to make films that were more left of field and less aimed at the main market. Films not with a principal goal of commerciality. Films that were made out of a desire to make a film about that and then think about the market. The films that were made at Rank were made for a machine, like the films made in Hollywood today. They were made to feed a marketplace and to be as successful as possible.

I remember the incredible experience of watching *Bridge on the River Kwai*, *Dr Zhivago* and *Lawrence of Arabia*. They were all great experiences in the cinema. And this conversation [about epiphanies] wouldn't be complete without the influence of *Citizen Kane*, which, even though everybody puts it at the top of their list, is the *Hamlet* of film. There is no denying that. I can't remember when I saw *Citizen Kane* first. It was probably at the National Film Theatre, but I saw it when I was young. It was like, wow! I examined it very closely with director Philippe Mora when I edited *Brother, Can You Spare a Dime?* We put the film up on a Steenbeck and we examined the film frame by frame. We cut some scenes for humour, which was very sacrilegious. But how all that stuff happened and came together, how they managed to do all those things in that story – the lighting, the acting, the story: they had a moment when the light shone and they made that incredible film. You can't beat it, it's unbeatable – masterly conjuring. I did encounter Orson Welles. On *Brother, Can You Spare a Dime?*, he edited the voiceover for the trailer. He came and did a trailer, which was 'The 30s were the great times and

Citizen Kane
(Orson Welles,
1941)

the bright times and I was there – you be there too.' He came and put this recording down. Afterwards, at the restaurant, I was there with a friend who knew him. I talked to him for a bit. He always had a project. His later film, F for Fake, was incredible – an incredible piece of conjuring for the cinema.

The films you see between the ages of eighteen and twenty-four are a powerful group of films. The films you see in that age group, at the time when you are making your mind up and people are helping you make your mind up, when you're debating films and not really read to pin your flag to the mast: these films inform and educate your later feelings about film. (I can tell immediately now when I don't like a film.) It was cool for me to be going to the National Film Theatre with a couple of friends. I was going there in the late 60s, when it was full of radical stuff going on. The LFF [London Film Festival] was radical. I'd go to the ICA. They were showing extraordinary stuff, much more than today. That was my impression.

I used to take the train up from the suburbs with friends to go to the NFT. That was a big outing. You felt you were in the know. You were anointed with knowledge that others didn't have. Those films we were seeing didn't come out in the local cinemas. In cinemas in Beaconsfield and Gerrards Cross, you didn't get films by Jean-Luc Godard. The manager had never heard of him. This was an era when there were three channels on TV. I do think that seeing films on telly is a much, much weakened version of seeing them in the cinema. It's a different experience. You can see incredible television but a movie in a cinema in a darkened house as a shared experience is never going to be duplicated at home.

Epiphanies? I could talk about a scene in Citizen Kane but it's not like that. It's a layering of film knowledge that has happened as you become aware. There is a mush at the beginning and then, as you become aware, it becomes clearer and clearer what you like and what you don't like. You become an instant critic yourself. **"**

Abbas Kiarostami

Eight and a Half

(Federico Fellini, 1963)

Kiarostami is one of Iran's leading film-makers and one of the most formally innovative directors currently working in world cinema. He won the Palme D'Or at Cannes for *The Taste of the Cherry* (1997). His work is characterised by its humanism, by the way it blurs the lines between documentary and fiction, and by its attention to landscape. His more recent films, notably *Ten* (2002) and *Five* (2003), have seen him pare down his storytelling aesthetic. His style might best be described as meditative minimalism.

Born in 1940 in Tehran, Kiarostami initially showed talent as an artist, attending the university's School of Fine Arts. While there, he supported himself by working as a traffic policeman. In the 1960s, he made advertisements for Iranian TV. His first feature, *Report*, was made in 1977.

Unlike many of his contemporaries, Kiarostami did not flee west after the Iranian revolution, choosing instead to continue living and working in the country. His early movies often featured children as the protagonists, and regularly exhibited a sly humour, notably in *Close-Up* (1990), his funny and poignant drama based on the real-life trial of a man who impersonated film-maker Mohsen Makhmalbaf. Kiarostami's films are both lyrical and rooted in the everyday. He is a paradoxical film-maker: seemingly a straightforward storyteller preoccupied with the everyday experiences of his characters but also formally innovative. Blurring fictional and non-fictional elements, his films also often have an allegorical undertow.

Geoffrey Macnab: What is your earliest memory of cinema?

Abbas Kiarostami: I think I was only ten when I first saw a film. It was the opening night of the first movie theatre in our neighbourhood. My older sister, who was fourteen years old, took me there. The first moving image we ever saw was the image of the MGM lion, which seemed quite scary to the boy I was then. I remember it as if it were only yesterday. The movie was about a man who played the piano with his nose. Later on, I was told that the man was Danny Kaye. Whoever he was, my sister and I left the theatre quite impressed; it felt like we were walking in the clouds. That's when I first discovered the magic power of the cinema

GM: Is there a single film you remember with special fondness from your childhood?

AK: I don't have any precise recollection concerning the movies from my early childhood. However, a few years later I fell in love with a film that was very different from anything else I'd seen back then. I really fell under the spell of *Eight and a Half*; that's why, as a smart, smooth move, I invited my girlfriend to the cinema, fantasising about the bond it would create between the two of us: a

relationship blessed by Fellini himself. It didn't quite turn out as I expected, however. As a matter of fact, during the screening, she wanted me to take her hand – but I didn't want to be disturbed or distracted in any way. We both left the theatre quite disappointed and unhappy, and never saw each other again. The theatre, incidentally, was called BB after the famous French movie star.

GM: Is there a single film that inspired you to want to become a film-maker?

AK: There wasn't a single movie, nor a single shot. It was a very slow but at the same time very effective process, which had contradictory aspects to it: Italian neo-realist films on the one hand, American Westerns on the other.

GM: How important an influence was Robert Bresson on your work?

AK: Well, I believe we have two Robert Bressons: Bresson the film-maker and Bresson the theorist. I have to confess I'm much more impressed by the theorist, even though I very much appreciate the film-maker. His films are courageous, unique and unforgettable. However, I am quite sure that he himself as a film-maker was a pupil to the theorist and also a follower of the same path. What

Eight and a Half

impresses me in his theory is how he promotes the dissociation between cinema on the one hand and theatre and literature on the other. This theory is so challenging and audacious that sometimes Bresson himself seems kind of 'dépassé'.

Being an adept of his theory meant encountering many difficulties in my work. But I am deeply convinced of the correctness – and the magic – of the idea of separating cinema from literature (or theatre). All his teaching leads us toward the elimination of anything that separates 'art' from 'movie business'. Jacques Rivette is right when he says that Bresson's testament to us is an ethical one.

GM: When you were at university studying fine arts, what kind of films were you watching? Did you have any idea that you yourself would become a film-maker?
AK: I was concentrating on trailers and short promotional films: either doing that or looking at other people's work.

Then I started to design credits and posters for films. In those days, I strongly believed that I had to work in whatever I was studying – but the truth of the matter was that I was not good at painting, my particular discipline at university. Therefore, I tried to take comfort from graphic works. I am sure that what I did in that area of work had its effect on the minimalist films I like to make today. I learned and appreciated how to say more with less – communicating through signs instead of using direct messages. In those days, I only watched the movies for which I had to make a poster or design the credits; furthermore, I only really concentrated on condensing a film's story in order to design the poster. So I couldn't actually afford to enjoy any of those movies; it was work and nothing else. Nevertheless, through that work I learned another way of looking at the world around me. I guess I already had it in me and I developed it over time, but as far as I was concerned, there was a story behind every single detail …

Terence Davies

Young at Heart

(Gordon Douglas, 1954)

Terence Davies on
the set of
*Distant Voices,
Still Lives* (1988)

The French revere British director Terence Davies and have long used him as a stick with which to hit their British counterparts. If Davies had been one of their own, they insist they would have nurtured his talent properly, ensuring that he made a new film every year as a matter of course. In the UK, Davies has had a tough time in securing financing for projects. At the time of writing (May 2009), he hasn't made a feature since his Edith Wharton adaptation *The House of Mirth* (2000). His brand of poetic and deeply personal film-making has sometimes seemed to belong to an earlier, more tolerant and imaginative era in British film culture. Davies emerged as a film-maker in the 1970s, at a time when such other directors as Bill Douglas, Derek Jarman, Sally Potter and Peter Greenaway were also being given the chance to make their first movies.

As a kid growing up in a working-class background in Liverpool, Davies has said, the idea that he might one day become a film-maker appeared impossibly far-fetched. In his 2008 documentary *Of Time and the City*, he revisits the Liverpool of his youth. Rather than a talking-heads documentary, full of polemic and statistics, this is a poetic meditation (Davies calls it 'a visual poem') in the vein of the great surrealist and documentary-maker Humphrey Jennings's *Listen to Britain*. Like all of Davies's work, it is about memory and loss. The film coincided with a revival in his career. The British Film Institute, which had supported him throughout his career, made him a 'Fellow' and also distributed *Of Time and the City*. Meanwhile, he was feted at festivals and was the subject of a retrospective at the National Film Theatre.

Critics have sometimes called Davies 'the proletarian Proust' and discussed the way he has 'wrenched high art from the lower depths of his deprived Liverpool childhood' in films like *Distant Voices, Still Lives* (1988) and *The Long Day Closes* (1992). At the risk of sounding patronising, such descriptions nonetheless hint at what makes Davies so special – his ability to reinvoke the past in a way that is both jolting and lyrical. In his work, family, religion, sexuality and memory are invariably foregrounded.

A disarming interviewee, he is articulate, gossipy, waspish and often very funny.

Terence Davies:

"I was taken by my elder sister to the movies to see *Singin' in the Rain*. It was the Odeon, London Road. Can you imagine what that felt like for a seven-year-old! In the 'Singin' in the Rain' number, I just wept and wept and wept and my sister said, why are you crying? I just couldn't stop crying. Every time I see it, I still cry. I was too young to appreciate Jean Hagen. She is utterly, utterly fabulous in it. It's a great comic performance – 'I earn more money than Calvin Coolidge … put together!'

It was such an extraordinary moment. It was like a great revelation. I never ever thought I would make films. People from working-class backgrounds didn't. You had to be posh and go to university. But it was one of the great revelations of my life. It opened up not so much cinema (because I was too young to understand that) but the possibility this world could exist. In the 50s, we thought America was like that. When he does 'Singin' in the Rain', it is inside a sound stage with false rain. It is! But we thought America was like that. Somebody described it as a state of mind. It wasn't. It was a place for the perfect. Little England was black and white. America was in colour.

The only time we were better was in comedy. There were a lot of picture houses near me – eight within walking distance. If you wanted to see a comedy, you went to see a British comedy. You didn't go to see Americans because they weren't very good. We had people like Margaret Rutherford, Alistair Sim, Joyce Grenfell, Terry-Thomas and a whole wonderful list of people who – as soon as they came on – you could feel waves of laughter toward the screen. You went to see American musicals, gangster films and what were called women's pictures. When I was eleven, my sister Helen said I am going to take you to the Forum on Sunday, in town. To be taken to the pictures in town! I can tell you, I couldn't concentrate on schoolwork all week. I just couldn't. It was to see Doris Day in *Young at Heart*. We got in just as the credits were beginning – fairy tales can come true and can happen to you. It was bliss. I fell in love with Doris Day instantly. These were all interiors. Even the street was an interior. You thought America was like that. Everyone lived in these perfect houses. They had big kitchens and wraparound teeth. It seemed paradise. You didn't come out thinking you were living in a Liverpool slum. You didn't. You came out thinking, oh, it's fabulous! I love that film

Young at Heart

still. Of all the Doris Day films, it's probably not her best but it is the one I love most. You begin to understand the acerbity of Frank Sinatra's performance.

A few months later, my two elder sisters took me to a performance of *Love Is a Many-Splendored Thing*. The same thing happened. We got the last three seats and they had to pay two and sixpence – an awful lot of money back then. It was a brilliant summer day. Again, everyone was weeping like everything except for the men, who didn't like films that made them cry – but they went anyway. Those were the three times, and I go back to them in my memory again and again. I can remember what route we took, where we sat. I can just remember it with such vividness. They had a huge effect on me.

I still have the same reaction to those Doris Day films. Those films are so powerful that as soon as I start, all my disbelief is completely suspended. I don't care if they are looking in the wrong place. I don't care. This is just joy. All my critical faculties go out of the window. Where *Love Is a Many-Splendored Thing* is concerned, you're aware it's not a great film but you're aware that in four shots, they are going to fall in love. That's not bad, in four shots. In *Young at Heart*, I can still see her coming in. It's a mid- to long shot. She's coming out of the kitchen. She is in a dressing gown. She is carrying milk. That's it! I just think, oh, isn't she fabulous! In her first shot in *The Pyjama Game* where she comes in in long shot, you just think that's a star! And she's very, very sexy! I say this as a gay man. And doesn't she look fabulous. What is it? I can't tell you. I can't analyse it, because in a way I don't want to because I love her so much.

They're actually two very dignified performances. There's a point where they come to the beach to swim. She says, I am seeing some people across the bay. Shall we swim there? Then they get in the water. That's the first time you hear 'Love Is a Many Splendored Thing'. That's it. I start to cry and I cry for the rest of the entire film, which is 60 minutes or something. I can't tell you why but that is the effect it has on me. I know how the shots are constructed, I know that it cuts from a real beach to a beach made in the studio but I don't care. I don't care. It's just fabulous. It reminds me of how I felt when I was ten or eleven. It reminds me that it was a communal event and that we all cried. I am still ten years old, watching it with my two sisters, sitting in between them, on a seat that cost two and sixpence.

In those days, they still had the seating like a theatre. With *Singin' in the Rain*, we sat in the orchestra stalls, halfway down on the right-hand side, on an aisle. With *Young at Heart*, my sister Helen wore a black costume suit with a little blouse that had a scallop neck. We got the last two seats in the 1*d* and 9*s*. When we came out, it was a hot evening and my sister felt faint. We walked halfway up London Road because we used to get a tram or a bus up Kensington Street. We stopped outside a shop called Grays where we had just bought a radiogram for 26 guineas. Then she didn't feel faint and we went home.

Where *Love Is a Many-Splendored Thing* is concerned, it was a Saturday matinee at 6.15pm and my two sisters Maisie and Eileen, we were the last people to get in and we went upstairs and just as we sat down, it started. It was in CinemaScope. As the curtain went back, the audiences gasped because it was CinemaScope.

Colour has an emotional effect on us. It does. That bright Technicolor. When you saw it was in colour, you were thrilled because most films were in black and white.

I wanted to be an actor originally and a writer. I joined the Liverpool writers' club which met every Tuesday, at 7.30pm. We all took our things along, read them out and people criticised them. I acted. I joined a little amateur dramatic society. Usually, I played in comedy. I played old men. Then, the shipping office where I worked closed down and I moved to an accountant's office, with the idea of becoming an accountant. I hated it but I was good at it. I acted more and more in the evening. I found a private tutor to give me acting lessons and applied to all the major drama schools in London – and never got in. So I thought, oh well, I can't be very good.

I used to buy *The Stage*. I think it came out every Thursday. I saw Coventry Drama School. I applied and I got in. While I was at my first year in drama school, I sent out the script to what was the first part of the trilogy. Everybody turned it down, so I thought it can't be any good. I used to go home once every three weeks. I was terribly homesick. I missed my mother so badly I can't tell you. I was looking forward to going home. There was a thing on TV on Friday night called *Cinema Now*. They had a programme on the BFI Production Board [which gave money to film-makers]. I sent my little script to the Production Board in Lower Marsh behind Waterloo. Three months later,

Mamoun Hassan, who was running the Production Board, said come down to London. I went down. He said, here's £8,500, not a penny more, you will direct. I said I hadn't directed. He said, now's your chance. It wouldn't happen now. Apart from the cameraman called Bill [William Diver], the rest of the crew hated the script, hated the way I directed and told me so the entire three weeks – it was awful. It was a baptism of fire. But you learned.

It would have been impossible to make films like the Doris Day musicals. We can't make them in this country. That kind of joie de vivre … even in my later films, you don't come out feeling the world is a wonderful place. You don't. I would have loved to have made *Young at Heart* or *Meet Me in St. Louis* or *Gypsy*, or any of those wonderful musi-cals. But I can't do that. I can't do it. It was such a traumatic experience making *Children* and I thought never again! It was so awful. I had to go back to drama school to finish my second year because if you didn't finish, you had to pay back your entire grant and I had no money. I felt that even though it was an awful experience, I remembered the magic of looking down the camera for the first time. I knew it was a trilogy. I mentioned this to Mamoun Hassan. He said he had just finished the Bill Douglas trilogy and didn't want to do another one. I went back to drama school, finished my second year, went back to Liverpool because I had to earn some money, went back to accountancy. I had such a sense of failure. I really did touch rock bottom. Then I applied to film school and I got in! **"**

Aki Kaurismäki

Nanook of the North

(Robert J. Flaherty, 1922)

Aki Kaurismäki can't do without his cigarettes. My interview was originally meant to take place in the offices of his UK distributor but when he learned of their no-smoking policy, we rapidly relocated to his hotel in Soho instead. 'You wouldn't want to make an interview with a character who is totally nervous about where he will get his next cigarette,' the Finnish director told me as he cracked open his first beer of the day. It was 10am.

Whatever his alcohol and nicotine consumption, Kaurismäki remains one of the few contemporary European film-makers whose work bears comparison with that of auteurs like Godard, Truffaut or – further back in time – his beloved Jean Vigo. He stands up for the oppressed. In his films, the heroes and heroines are invariably small-timers who have been betrayed. Their lovers may have left them. Their bosses may have sacked them. They teeter on the edge of despair but the director (who has described himself as 'an old man with a tender heart') generally engineers some kind of final-reel redemption for them.

Kaurismäki is a poet of the oppressed. Early in his career, he had his share of dead-end jobs, working as a postman and dishwasher. In films from *Ariel* (1988) to *Drifting Clouds* (1996), he has focused on characters at the bottom of the social ladder, battling unemployment, broken hearts and alcoholism. There is a hint of Charlie Chaplin (albeit without the sentimentality) in many of his protagonists: security guards, laid-off workers, amnesiac down-and-outs and suicidal clerks. Alongside the Chaplinesque elements, there is also a strong Dostoevskian strain to his work. His first film as a director was a reworking of *Crime and Punishment* (1983) set in present-day Helsinki. His 1990 masterpiece *The Match Factory Girl*, about a downtrodden factory worker with a vengeful streak, also owed an obvious debt to the Russian novelist. In the ingenious *Hamlet Goes Business* (1987), he reworked Shakespeare's tragedy, setting it in present-day Finland against a backcloth of corporate skulduggery. Instead of Elsinore, we are in the offices of a company that mass-manufactures rubber ducks. The conceit might verge on kitsch but, amid the bath toys, Kaurismäki still manages to retain the brooding intensity of the play.

A co-founder of the Midnight Sun Festival, which takes place every year close to the Arctic Circle during midsummer (at a time when the sun never sets), Kaurismäki is – or used to be – a dedicated cinephile. It's his boast, but also his lament, that he has already seen everything in world cinema that is worth seeing.

Aki Kaurismäki:

"I have the moment [of epiphany]. I can tell you the date and the films. It was the end of March in '73. I was sixteen years old and I was a member of a film club. I was very keen on surrealism at that time and I heard about a film called *L'Âge d'or* by Buñuel. I wanted to go to see that but of course, I was late. The idea of surrealism I had was different. I didn't know that this was a double bill and they had chosen *Nanook of the North* by Robert Flaherty as the first film. Then, after that, they showed *L'Âge d'or* and I loved them both. Until this moment, I had seen every shit I could but this woke me up to understand that cinema can be art. I remember I was in shock. I went around the little village where I lived saying, 'This is great', but nobody understood what the hell I was talking about. They haven't understood since. I am a child of film clubs. I would never have known cinema without film clubs.

And there was *A Matter of Life and Death*. I had the honour to meet Mr Powell in my life. As a film-maker, I am totally the opposite of Mr Powell. He came to the Midnight Sun Festival in 1987. Pressburger I never met. I never had money so I can't spend too much. But I admire the way Powell used the money he had. To make a stairway to heaven [as Powell did] would be nice but I don't have time to wait for them to make the stairs. I spent my youth seeing British films. They were shown on television all the time. I saw all the Alec Guinness films and that formulated my picture of English society. I thought the British were the guys who won the war.

I was from a middle-class background but how can you write a ballad for the middle class? I don't mean that they don't have troubles, like everyone else, but the dialogue is impossible because they are trapped. We are trapped in the middle class. It's easy to be a slave or a boss but it's hard to be in the middle. You have to take care of your family in a certain way. It's hard to make a revolution. That is why I made the films I did. I always had my eyes open. I was always watching how people feel when they are fired."

Nanook of
the North

SCREEN EPIPHANIES

A Matter of
Life and Death
(Michael Powell,
1946)

Stephen Frears

*Morgan: A Suitable
Case for Treatment*

(Karel Reisz, 1966)

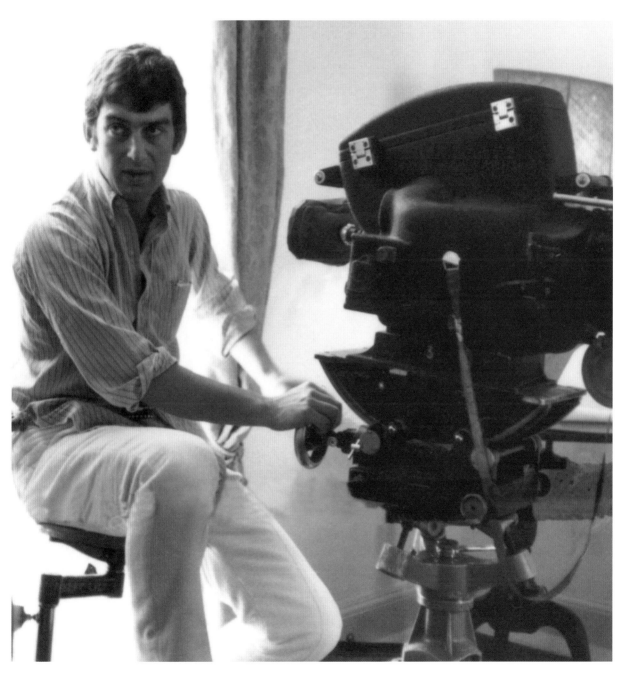

Stephen Frears on
the set of *The
Burning* (1968)

Actress Michelle Pfeiffer, who worked with Stephen Frears on *Dangerous Liaisons* (1988) and *Chéri* (2009), described the way the British director 'walks around the set with this Detective Columbo personality, mumbles around and acts as if he doesn't know what is going on and is confused about everything'. His gruff persona, Pfeiffer pointed out, belies the fact that he is a sharp and perceptive film-maker who knows exactly what he wants. Interviewing Frears in his Notting Hill kitchen, one has a sense of what Pfeiffer is talking about.

Frears's filmography is as long and varied as that of his contemporaries, Mike Newell and Michael Apted. He has made Westerns (*The Hi-Lo Country*, 1998), films about disaffected British teens (*Bloody Kids*, 1979), one of Britain's first gay-themed mainstream hits (*My Beautiful Laundrette*, 1985) and a very well-received drama about the British Royal Family in the wake of Princess Diana's death (*The Queen*, 2006).

Frears was born in 1941 in Leicester to a middle-class family. His mother was a social worker and his father was a doctor. As he recounts below, he didn't set out to become a film-maker but slowly edged his way into the industry after leaving Cambridge University in the early 1960s. His career is marked by a long hiatus between his first feature, *Gumshoe* (1971), and his re-emergence as a movie director in the mid-1980s. For much of the 1970s and early 80s, he was working in television, which attracted the best writing and offered the opportunity to make films. The success of *My Beautiful Laundrette*, which was made for the small screen but eventually released in cinemas, galvanised his career. Since then, he has worked in Britain and in Hollywood. He has a reputation as an insightful and reliable craftsman who can turn his hand to almost anything.

Stephen Frears:

"I remember when television arrived in the late 50s. We didn't have television in the late 40s. When we moved to Nottingham, the people next door had a television. I can remember watching the England v. Hungary game there. And I remember things like at school going to see the Cup Final. But there were forty cinemas in Leicester. I mean, it was non-stop. The more seedy cinemas, the suburban cinemas, would change the programme halfway through the week and there would be a different programme on Sunday anyway. There was nothing else to do except go to the pictures. I can remember being taken to see *Pinocchio*. I mainly went with my mother. My father was away, first in the war and then studying medicine. I spent a lot of time with my mother. She used to take me to the cinema to see what I expect were rather unsuitable films. I can remember seeing *The Way to the Stars*. I sort of grew up on adult films in some rather odd way – there were an awful lot of submarines. There weren't really American films. There was one called *Son of Sherwood Forest*, but I don't know if that was English or American. American films didn't really come in until the end of the 40s. I can remember *Red River* coming in. My mother was very keen on seeing *Red River* and I didn't want to. I didn't want to see it because I would have wanted to see some British piece of nonsense. We used to go to a cinema in Leicester which was next door to where they have the circus and you could hear the lions roaring.

My wife when I met her, which was in the 60s, I told her I worked with a really good editor. She thought film only existed on a large screen and the quality that made a good editor was the ability to cut straight across the bottom of the screen with a pair of scissors. She thought that was what editing was. My ex-wife was an extremely intelligent woman. Films weren't made. They were just seen. There was no sense of films being made.

There were books, odd things like *Picturegoer Annual*, but the idea that films were made was inconceivable. Then I went away to school in 1949 – a prep school in Warwickshire. They used to show a film every weekend, on Saturday afternoon, and then they'd show it again on Sunday. It was a way of controlling the children. It was a sort of concentration camp. They will all be watching the film – we've got them locked in for two hours. They would show 16mm prints and there would be reel breaks. I saw a lot of largely British films. I could tell you all about *I See a Dark Stranger*. The Marx brothers films they would show. I remember a lot of Will Hay films and George Formby, I think. I remember a lot of Tommy Trinder films and they showed the Michael Wilding films (*Spring in Park Lane* and *Maytime in Mayfair*). I know all that stuff. And I remember liking Basil Radford and Naunton Wayne and then, I guess, Ealing comedies. Ealing comedies always seem the best – the classiest stuff. I have quite a detailed knowledge about British films of that period. I don't think there was any question of not seeing it. They didn't show *The Third Man* or anything like that. *49th Parallel* I remember. In other words, there was a heroic or comic view of British life which they supported and was part of the ethos. There were a lot of escape films, prisoner-of-war films – *The Wooden Horse* and *Colditz*. *The Cruel Sea*, *Genevieve*. Am I nostalgic? If I see it, I burst into tears. It is so imprinted on your mind. I was a middle-class boy. They [the characters in the films] were romantic versions of the world I was brought up in.

My father had become a doctor after the war. He was a chartered accountant. We were small-business people. My brother went into the family business, which then got taken over and he became an academic. My other brother became a neurologist. I had two older brothers. I can remember my brother taking the family to a rather obscure cinema in Nottingham and we saw *High Noon*. That would have been some time in the mid-50s. And I remember seeing *North by Northwest*. Then, of course, came films about the cities I was living in and the world changed. My brother told me about Marlon Brando and took me to *On the Waterfront*. I loved *The Crimson Pirate* and asked to be taken back. *Samson and Delilah* was the same.

There was certainly no indication that this was going to be my life's work. I studied law because I was the child of professional people. I didn't want to become a doctor because I was squeamish and so I became a lawyer. I should have done history but I had an appalling history teacher who destroyed my interest. I was acting in school plays. The son of an actor was at school and I went to stay with him. Then I must have met Lindsay [Anderson] in 1960. I met him privately because I went to stay with the family of this friend of mine in Majorca. [The actor] Daniel Massey was there too and Lindsay was trying to persuade Dan to be in *Sergeant Musgrave's Dance*.

Lindsay was a very impressive person but by then, I was starting to become interested in the Royal Court and the New British Cinema. It was a good time to be young.

I must have been about eighteen when I met Lindsay. Then I went up to Cambridge where there were people like [the academic and writer] Charles Barr writing. There was a cinema club at Cambridge. I can remember seeing *La Règle du jeu* there. There was an art cinema in Cambridge that used to show a masterpiece every week – endless Bergman and all those European films that came out at that time. I was a young, thrusting intellectual, as it were. I was an undergraduate and the films were part of the language of the time in a way that they are not now. You had endless arguments and discussions about *L'avventura* or *Hiroshima, mon amour*. I can remember taking a girl to see *Rocco and His Brothers*. I saw *Shoot the Pianist* and *Jules and Jim*. With British films, you just knew that something new was happening. *Room at the Top* was about provincial people. *Saturday Night, Sunday Morning* was about working-class people. My brother was an extra in it. It was about a city that I recognised. The cinema had begun to be about a world I understood and found interesting

rather than about Kenneth More. Now, young people are all interested in music but at the time, they were interested in film. This was pre-Beatles and pre the obsessiveness with which young people now know about music. I was just part of that social revolution in Britain. I'd come down to London and hung around at the Court. It just seemed so interesting. The people were so vivid. I'd never seen *O Dreamland*. My interest was in the Court and then spun off into the films that people from the Court made and that were made from plays that had been done there – all that stuff that came to be known as 'kitchen sink'. Anderson was talking about John Ford the whole time. There was a lot of talk about Gladys Henson in *The Blue Lamp* being told that Jack Warner has been shot. We used to imitate that a great deal. 'I'll just put these in water,' she says to Jimmy Hanley. What I loved was a film of Carol Reed called *The Way Ahead*.

The first director I ever met was Guy Hamilton. He was on holiday one time when I went on holiday to Majorca with this friend of mine. I gave up law when I finished at Cambridge and ended up working at the Court. Then I met Karel Reisz. He came to do a play. Meeting him was what really changed my life.

He came to do a play and Lindsay said, 'oh, you should have Stephen', and I was going to work on it. Then, he couldn't cast the play or something and the play collapsed. Karel said, you better come and work on my film, which was *Morgan: A Suitable Case for Treatment*. I went to work on his film. I had never been on a film set before. Betsy, his widow, said he came home one day and said he had a very bright chap who was going to be his assistant. I don't know why he said that. That was more epiphany-forming than anything else.

Karel was a wonderful man, a fantastic human being, graceful and human. He was a family man. Lindsay was much more obviously an artist. Karel valued his family because he had lost his family in the war and he had lost his country afterward. He had had bad times. The truth is I don't really remember anything except being in a mess the whole time. All I wanted really to do was find out who I was or what I was going to do for the rest of my life. It was as though you were trying to work out what kind of peg you are and then find the kind of hole that you go into. It wasn't as if I really wanted to make a film. I just wanted to sort myself out. Seeing Karel, I just thought this is a very nice man and this is a very nice life. He

Morgan: A Suitable Case for Treatment

had values that I rather admire. It was his family and him as a human being. I don't think he was idiotically rich or anything like that. I just really remember the confusion. Then I went to work for Albert [Finney] and made a little film in Tangier [*The Burning*] about South Africa and I started getting work. I started getting hired as a director for television. Then I went on from there. It was never 'oh, I really want to make a film', the way that people talk about it now. I just wanted to sort out who I was.

I started making children's films and then I met this chap called Neville Smith and we wrote *Gumshoe*. I started getting to know people like Ken Loach and Tony Garnett and began to know what my generation was doing and what it was interested in. So it was really just following certain people. Alan Bennett I got to know. I followed him because he was so interesting. He was great friends with the woman I then married. Then I ended up doing the first films he scripted. I made a film [*Gumshoe*] before I was thirty. You would think that was the mark of someone with a very clear sense of where they were going. Quite the opposite! I thought *Gumshoe* was wonderful, the script was brilliant, but there was no sense of purpose in my life. There was a

muddled ambition. I never knew what I was supposed to be doing. I could easily have gone off in another direction. Afterwards, you think that God was very kind. He steered you to where you were at home.

I had been rejected by Granada as not good enough. There were no film schools but the TV companies used to come and recruit at Cambridge. I applied and I can remember going for the same scheme as Mike Apted and Michael Newell. They got the jobs and I didn't. So the Royal Court was my apprenticeship. I had an old-fashioned apprenticeship I now see. In retrospect, I was like a golden child. I was very privileged. I was literally attached to these men. I was like a pupil of Michelangelo. Lindsay and Karel changed my life. Nobody will believe me but it all came as a big surprise to me, making films.

I don't know what they liked about me. They're both dead and so you'll never find out. Karel always said I was a very good assistant. I have no idea why. I worked on *If* .... . By then I was a film director. On *If* ...., I was a hanger-on. I always thought the film was wonderful from the first day I read it, and interesting. I did all the collages. I cut the pictures out for all the collages in the boys' rooms. We were cutting stuff out about students confronting authority at the same time that we were shooting the scenes at Cheltenham of students confronting authority. We couldn't have been more aware of its topicality. The headmaster knew perfectly well what was going on. He was a clever man. He knew Lindsay was up to mischief. I liked that abrasiveness of Lindsay Anderson. I presumably have a certain amount of that in me.

I had started directing plays at Cambridge. Influenced by the Royal Court and knowing that I was no good as an actor or a writer, that [directing] was what I was interested in. Then I worked with Karel on *Morgan*. Then I was passed like a parcel to Albert Finney and worked on *Charlie Bubbles*.

In the middle of the 80s, I woke up. I had got into television through Alan [Bennett], who wasn't in the mainstream, but was cleverer than anyone else. He wasn't writing extreme left-wing plays or any nonsense like that. I became one of the directors that the BBC supported without being aware of it. They backed certain people. I was again so privileged. I am embarrassed to describe how I learned to make films to people, it was so comfortable! You learned by making films. None of us knew what to do. By making two or

Lindsay Anderson
on the set of
If .... (1968)

three films a year, you just learned. One year I made four films in a row and kept an office. Nobody could work out how I did it. The BBC was commissioning at a high rate and it was commissioning the best writers in Britain. It was like standing at the neck of a bottle. The stuff had to go through this gorge and we were there waiting to direct it. I was one of the chosen ones. The drama got huge audiences. It will never have that good a time again. That is kind of where the problem is. In the war, British film-making had a subject. Television found this subject of the new Britain, post-war Britain, and it was very, very interesting. Now, it doesn't have a subject. At the time, it had an absolute specific subject – it was the 60s and 70s, all the result of social changes in the 40s. It was really the post-war reckoning. Mrs Thatcher tried to turn the clock back and say that was all terrible, but in fact it was extremely interesting.

At the end of the 70s, what was happening was that unbeknown to us, Thatcher was deregulating. That changed the mood. Suddenly, ITV companies realised that if they put money into film, they could get it off tax. And so they suddenly started making much more expensive films [for television]. I remember Jack Gold making an expen-

sive film for Thames and I made *Bloody Kids* for ATV. It was much more expensive – much more money than we had ever had.

It [working for TV] was very, very protected. That's good news and bad news, always. You make a film now and it involves a lot of money. Part of your heart sinks. Somehow, it [television] wasn't as under pressure. I grew up under the welfare state and I've had to work out how to live under capitalism.

Ken Loach had a huge influence on me but I also remember somehow not wanting to be influenced by him, resisting it quite actively. Ken was a wonderful film-maker. He had such a powerful influence. He was such a huge presence. It [resistance] was just general rebelliousness on my behalf. Alan Clarke I can remember discovering standing over me in the cutting room, saying how did you do that shot? I said, well there's a thing called a Steadicam. Buggered if he was a pioneer! He was just copying what Chris [Menges] and I had done on a film called *Walter*.

With *My Beautiful Laundrette*, I was rung up and told that this boy wanted to get a script to me. A script came through the letterbox. I read the script and my heart sank because I realised it was about Pakistanis and then I started to laugh. Then he came to see me. Hanif turned up here, in this room. I thought he was somebody else. I can remember saying, you think that people like me are just ridiculous old liberals. And he said, I like ridiculous old liberals. It was completely fortuitous, but I must have been ready to do it. I had always been the youngest person on a film, the boy, and suddenly I was the oldest person on this film. I couldn't pass myself off as a child any more. I knew when I read *My Beautiful Laundrette* that it was good but I didn't think it would have the future it had.

I was always just a working director but the work more often than not was on something interesting.

In the films I saw as a child, there was no footprint. The films might have been good and vivid but the idea of the director was of no importance at all. We all really predate that moment when film-making became self-conscious. You didn't think about style. The Royal Court was a writer's theatre. Television was a writer's medium. Your job was to service. You might do it gracefully, elegantly and well but it wasn't to usurp the role of the writer. I am a director. I can only direct what somebody has written – it has to be written first. I was just sent a few scripts I liked. That has happened to me all my life, more or less. I suppose there were no epiphanies. Meeting Karel Reisz and Lindsay Anderson was a human epiphany as opposed to a 'going to the movies' epiphany. And meeting Kureishi was an epiphanic moment – I'd be better under 'interesting people I have met'. **"**

Mike Figgis

Weekend

(Jean-Luc Godard, 1967)

Mike Figgis came from an experimental tradition in music and theatre. As a teenager, he played in a band with Bryan Ferry (later of Roxy Music). Figgis had his own theatre group and was passionately interested in jazz and art. What his career as a film director has made clear is how inflexible and conservative the film business can be. An industry that deals in 90–120-minute narrative features wasn't always particularly interested in the more radical work Figgis championed. Although some of his early features, for example the noirish, Newcastle-set gangster film *Stormy Monday* (1988) or the brilliant cop thriller *Internal Affairs* (1990), may have seemed mainstream, this was not territory that Figgis was likely to inhabit for long.

Figgis is an actor's director. As he showed in *Leaving Las Vegas* (1995), for which Nicolas Cage won an Oscar for his performance as the alcoholic, self-destructive screenwriter, and in his Strindberg adaptation *Miss Julie*, he has an ability to elicit searing performances from his leads. On the other hand, the British director is more interested in form (and in how it marries with technology) than almost any of his contemporaries. While other film-makers shied away from digital, he embraced it wholeheartedly. Whether it is using split screen, experimenting with sound design or embracing the no-budget Dogme aesthetic, he is always ready to take the most radical and challenging route.

Born in Carlisle in 1948, Figgis grew up in Kenya in the dying days of British colonial rule. His mother was briefly a secretary to Ernest Hemingway. Eventually, his family moved to the north of England. The Hemingway influence can be felt in his autobiographical film *The Loss of Sexual Innocence* (1999), which in parts plays like a north-east England-set version of Hemingway's Nick Adams stories.

Mike Figgis:

"I grew up in Nairobi till I was eight. The first film I ever saw was the Coronation film. I remember being taken into Nairobi by my mother to see the film of the Coronation. That was the only film I ever recollect seeing till I came back to Carlisle when I was eight. Then my cousins started to take me to matinees. I saw things like *Hopalong Cassidy*, science-fiction films, things like that. Then my grandmother got a television, sometime in the early 60s. I remember seeing *The Spiral Staircase*. That stayed with me.

My exposure to alternative cinema came about because I had a girlfriend who worked as an usher, part time, in the Tyneside Film Theatre, which was the closest thing in Newcastle to an art-house cinema. I guess I was about seventeen. It must have been 1965 or something. I got free entrance into the cinema when she was working. I remember clearly seeing a film called *Herostratus* by Don Levy which I'd love to see again. It was the first film I had ever seen that had played with the form and that wasn't a strictly linear narrative. There are a couple of images I can still remember. Then I went down to London to college. There was a film club there and there were a couple of films I saw. One was *The Incident at Owl Creek*, the short film, which I have watched again and which holds up pretty strongly. It was a completely silent narrative and was very arty – very artily crafted. *The Round-Up* – I remember seeing that at the film club at Trent Park College and being very taken by that. But I guess the two films that really turned me round were *Bonnie and Clyde* and *Weekend*.

I remember going to see *Bonnie and Clyde* when it came out at the cinema and being completely blown away by the style of the film, its humour and its violence. That film has stayed with me. I would put it certainly in my top five films. But Godard's *Weekend* was such a dynamic revelation for me. It was complete accident that led me to it. It was on. I didn't know who Jean-Luc Godard was.

My regime normally with films is that if I see a really good film, I have no desire to see it again. I like to live with the memory of it. I have watched *Bonnie and Clyde* a couple of times and I've watched *Weekend* a couple of times. I also did the introduction on the last DVD release of *Weekend* and so I had to watch it again. I presented it at the French Institute to quite a young audience, talked about it, then watched it on a print that was very, very distressed. I had seen it before on a pretty good DVD that was clean. Watching it in a cinema was like watching an old film

Bonnie and Clyde
(Arthur Penn,
1967)

because the print was old. When you watch it on DVD, you don't have the imposition of the wear and tear on the print and it seems like a completely modern, contemporary film that as far as I am concerned could have been made at any time. I think the ideas are still radical, revolutionary and bold when compared with what is around in the cinema right now. The style is avant-garde compared to what passes as the avant-garde now. I loved the cinematography. I loved – and still love – his use of music. I love the irony of the cartoon characterisation of the bourgeois characters. It has got one of the best sex scenes of any film I've ever seen, maybe because it is ironic and a clever pastiche parallel to Bataille's *Story of the Eye*. The film is incredibly funny, ironic and smart. It's both innovative and political. As a document of its time, it's a priceless piece of documentation. As a film in its own right, I find it immensely enjoyable. There are elements that when I am writing or when I am making a film are very present in my understanding of what cinema is. There are amazing moments in all of his films, including his later films, but before *Weekend*, I hadn't seen other films in which these things were done with such humour. I was studying music when I was at college. I was very taken by Godard's use of

music and by the realisation that the music was a tool being used as part of his ironic overview.

I wasn't at all thinking of myself as a potential film-maker. The thing I loved about Godard was that his sensibility was very sympathetic to the idea of experimental theatre. I was using music, deconstructed narrative [in my theatre work]. Most of the other films I saw were conventional, narrative films. What I liked about Godard was that he wasn't so many miles away from the leaders of the avant-garde theatre or performance-art movement. His work, that of Francis Bacon, Magritte and people like that was influential on the work that we were doing. At that point, it didn't cross my mind to be a film-maker because I was perfectly happy with what we were doing in this performing-arts context. I didn't think of Godard as cinema. I just thought of him as an interesting visual artist.

If you cut to a couple of years later, I started using film, a Super-8mm camera, in terms of a mixed-media approach to performance. I had filmed a few arty things. I thought it would be interesting to learn about film-making. So I decided to try to go to the National Film School, take three years out and learn something new. But I didn't get in. I was pissed off. I had submitted some

Super-8mm home-movie footage that I had shot and some very evolved sound-design tapes that I had been making in the context of the work I was doing. I remember being outraged when I discovered at my interview that they had actually played the tapes and showed the home movies at the same time. That would have turned the home movies into a kind of David Lynch landscape. There was no relationship between the two. I asked why they had been run at the same time. One was a home movie. The other was serious work that I had been doing for the last ten years. The interview went really, really badly from then on in. I think they were deeply suspicious. That confirmed a lot of my feelings about cinema. They were so suspicious of performance art and the art world. For them, a film was a film and the crossover is not possible. I didn't get into the film school, which made me extremely angry. I felt I was totally qualified along their terms for what they said they were looking for. I went off and made a film anyway.

I started to try to make a film on 16mm, applying some Godardian ideas. That seemed suitable language for cinema to me. Being a musician, I was very obsessed and fascinated by how to use music in film. I always felt that Godard had a better understanding of music than any other film-maker around. Most people use music to parallel and enhance a conventional emotional idea. I am sad – let's play some sad music. I am scared – let's play some atonal, dissonant music because we know that works in a scary way. It's a big landscape – let's play big landscape music. It's almost like idiot definitions that repeat over and over again in all films. Godard was ahead of his time in terms of Dogme film-making. In *Weekend*, there is a concert pianist playing Mozart in a barnyard in a farm. In another film, there is a string quartet rehearsing a Beethoven quartet. In *Le Mépris*, he pretty much uses one piece of music and repeats it over and over again. The music starts to compound in terms of its apparent significance. In *Weekend* during the sexual monologue at the beginning of the film, he occasionally drowns out the monologue by bringing in a very dark piece of music and you don't know what she is saying. Ironically, in the British release, they subtitle what she is saying. That puts us at a slight advantage over the French audience, who can't hear it. Godard is entirely disrespectful of the convention of the dynamic that the score normally incorporates – that it is a subscore, there to enhance things or occasionally to make a big noise because nothing else is happening. Godard,

Weekend

though, sees the music as an independent voice. And he loves music. He – of all film-makers – understands that the emotional response to a piece of music in the brain is entirely different to the visual brain response. If you can play the two against each other, then you are confusing in such an interesting way. It's not just parallel narrative. It's a parallel and diverse emotion that you are dealing with. I don't know another film-maker who understands music that well – well enough to articulate his tools in that way. He is clearly a very clever person. Occasionally, his cleverness alienates the audience, in that he makes cruel cinema. But like all great intellectuals, if you are prepared to see the film on his terms, then it will always be a fulfilling experience. Clearly, his brain still functions really well. His intellectual personality continues to shine. Even in the last couple of films that I have seen, that were really hard to watch, if you're prepared to engage from the beginning to the end of the piece, it will give you something.

I was putting myself out and about at the time [of *Weekend*], discovering the cultural scene. I remember seeing Peter Brook's version of *US*, an anti-Vietnam protest play that was an RSC production, in which Glenda Jackson made a very impassioned speech saying she would love to see a bomb go off in an Oxford tea party and see scattered limbs for people to understand. I remember thinking that was a terribly moving speech. Then, you see Godard. It's on the borderline between irony and cynicism. I don't think it was cynical because he was a very politically committed person. You understand that art is not fund-raising documentary. It is comment. The function of the true artist is to comment artistically. At the end of the day, a bunch of actors on the RSC stage pretending to be activists – OK, Glenda Jackson was an actress – the realisation that the contract for the suspension of disbelief is interesting, fragile – and one has to be always aware of where it sits in your political perspective. It is only a play. It is only a film. The irony and the humour that was apparent to me even at a young age in Godard's work was something I found very comfortable. I got the message but I didn't feel I was being preached to by a Hampstead left-wing liberal bourgeois intelligentsia. The delicious irony that Godard employed. As a comment on its time, Godard is one of the few film-makers who doesn't have flared trousers, if you know what I mean. When I presented the film at the French Institute, even though the print was completely buggered and made it seem like an old movie, there were jump-cuts and things like that in it that I had forgotten. In a way, the obvious things like the famous shot of the traffic accident were less interesting. It was nice to see them. They were like old friends. But there were things I had completely forgotten that seemed very radical – and would be totally acceptable in a radical film-maker right now. He had survived the flared-trouser test – even if some of the actors were wearing flared trousers.

Wasn't Godard invited initially to make *Bonnie and Clyde* and then in the end didn't do it? There was a real crossover. Funnily enough, I'm very good friends with John Boorman. When you see things like *Point Blank*, that's such a modern film. It's so experimental. It's Tarantino eat your heart out – it's pop art, *nouvelle vague* and all those things.

There was an interesting group of film-makers just as there was an interesting group of musicians at the time. You could definitely see that everyone was listening to everyone else. There is a real movement forward because there is that 60s energy in terms of the culture moving forward. It's really interesting. They were cousins, those films. I've kept the letter of rejection from the BFI for my first short film, which was the *nouvelle vague* version of *Stormy Monday* in 12 minutes. It was called *Mindless Violence*. It was about an execution that took place in

that location – Newcastle, going down a very steep hill to the river. I think it must have been influenced by *One Plus One*. This idea of a very stylised, choreographed execution. I think Bryan Ferry was the person I was suggesting being executed, wearing a white suit. Some kind of pop figure was being taken down by two gangsters and shot and thrown into the river. It was the journey down the hill and the people he passed. It was an ironic comment on what was perceived as the culture of the time. I remember the letter. It said, 'Dear Mike, while we find some visual interest in your script, we find it to be politically vacuous. With regret, we're turning down your request to be funded by the BFI.' I kept the letter.

I was very good friends with Walter Donahue, who has been a really good mentor to me over the years. I knew him from the Royal Court when he was an adviser there and he had been in on the early days of Channel 4. Through my connection with Walter, I got my first film, *The House*, made and then a few years later got *Stormy Monday* made. I remember him giving me some advice – if you want to make a film, shoot in London so you can make it within 10 miles of Bar Italia. You won't incur any extra expenses for travelling. I remember a list. It should be this and it should be this because that is the only thing that will get funded here.

I set out, tailor-made, to write this script based on those limited rules. It was called 'How to Make a Movie'. I became aware there was this gulf between the work I had been doing in the theatre, which had absolutely no censorship and you just did it, and the cinema. I knew there was an audience because I had been doing the *People Show* [an experimental British theatre group] for ten years and they were a very, very popular group, in England and abroad. Then to come across this British film establishment really was like visiting your auntie in terms of their conservative attitude. This was epitomised by Alexander Walker. He always referred to Godard in the TV guide of the *Evening Standard* as 'the great French bore'. There was this unbending attitude of never finding anything redeeming. It was never 'it's not for me but clearly the guy is interesting'. It was 'he's a bore, this is pretentious. This is not real cinema.' And that's what I came up against. It was really frustrating.

I have a feeling that meeting Godard would be a real mistake. I've interviewed Raoul Coutard on stage at the ICA. I've written extensively about Godard and am unashamedly a fan. Some of that may have filtered back to him, but who knows?

I loved his fascination with American cinema and his knowledge. He was almost like a Tarantino figure. He absorbed so much of that culture. I didn't. I never had the time or the inclination to watch every Vincente Minnelli film. My knowledge of cinema is pathetic. I have great knowledge of music and jazz and the other art forms, probably more than cinema. I find a lot of it terribly time-consuming. I never wanted to be a student of cinema in that respect. However, the pervasive quality of collective cinema that seeps through the cracks of everything is something that you're very aware of in film. You only need to see a couple of films from each period to get it. It's a bit like music. If you look at the back catalogue of jazz, it starts off very small because there weren't a lot of things being recorded. It grows very, very quickly through technology. By the time you get to the 50s, the catalogue has gone crazy. When are you going to find the time to listen to all that stuff. I've had that time to listen to it and be selective because I knew what I was looking for. It's a little bit the same with cinema.

Godard had said to camera manufacturers Aaton, I want you to design a camera that is small enough for me to carry in the glove compartment of my car so that if I see something, I can just stop and shoot it. I subsequently met the guy from Aaton. He said it was frustrating. He'd work on stuff and then go and visit Godard on the set of a film in Paris but Godard then wouldn't have time to talk to him. He felt a little bit he had been neglected. Then Aaton developed the Super-16mm camera. That was revolutionary. It brought Aaton into a potential feature-film-making role. I think it was called the Minima. It was truly small. Then, video comes along and Aaton is in deep trouble. It looks like Super-16mm might be going out of business. Then, it looks like film might be going out of business. Godard made a film in which half was on video and half on film.

In a way, I've much more enjoyed Godard's Americana than the actual thing that he is referring to. Von Trier's *Dogville* just annoyed the hell out of me because I felt it wasn't informed enough in a way. I had a feeling that Godard's mind was much more interesting to me – what he had absorbed and regurgitated through things like *Made in the USA* and *Alphaville*, which was a masterpiece of ironic homage. Whereas *Dogville* was kind of brattish and clichéd. I've seen *Dogville* done so much better by the Wooster Group or performance-art groups. They have dealt with that idea of minimal sets. After seeing *Weekend*, I didn't then go on a mission and think I must see what this guy has done.

I have always had the feeling that with very creative people, they often go through that rather self-righteous period. Often with musicians, they find God or they find music in the East and God at the same time. You think, OK, we're in for a slightly more introspective period as they discover their roots. But then they'll eventually do an album called 'Plays Ballads'. That's OK. You allow great artists, and even encourage them, to indulge themselves. That's what they do. They won't find out anything otherwise. I was aware of the fact that in the period of Godard's career where he turned to Maoism, one started to hear that he was no longer a director as he went through this whole Marxist re-evaluation of the role of the artist. There may be a period where you might suspend your sense of humour or your irony. Politics sometimes has that effect on artists. I wasn't so involved in his work in that period. But then, things like *Passion* and *First Name Carmen* started to come out – and the *Hail Mary* one. I watched all of them and there were always interesting ideas. You might be a little bit bored in the film but you know there are going to be things in it that you think about afterwards. Certainly by then, if you're making films, you're thinking how did he do that? He is always a talent, always provocative and always so inspiring. "

Mira Nair

La Jetée

(Chris Marker, 1962)

Mira Nair filming
The Namesake
(2006)

Indian film-maker Mira Nair made a spectacular entrance as a film-maker with *Salaam Bombay!* (1988). A film about street kids in Bombay, it had a documentary realism evocative of post-war Italian cinema as well as a vivid quality – a humour and liveliness amid the poverty – that seemed positively Dickensian. Since then, she has worked in India, Britain and America. She has made literary adaptations (a version of Thackeray's *Vanity Fair*, 2004), comedy-dramas set in the new India (*Monsoon Wedding*, 2001), stories about love across ethnic lines (*Mississippi Masala*, 1991) and a study of Indian first-generation immigrants in the US (*The Namesake*, 2006). Whatever form she is working in, her films invariably have a freewheeling zest about them.

Nair was born in 1957 in Rourkela, Orissa, into a middle-class Hindu family. Her father, Nayyar She, was a civil servant and her mother a social worker. Nair went on to study sociology at Delhi University. For several years, she was part of an amateur dramatic company. Then, in 1976, she won a scholarship to Harvard to study for a liberal arts degree and subsequently began her film-making career directing documentaries.

Mira Nair:

"I came to Cambridge, Massachusetts, on a scholarship at Harvard when I was nineteen from Orissa, a very small town in India. I didn't really see films there. When I was at university in Delhi, it was pretty much solidly theatre. There was the occasional romantic Bollywood movie but nothing I took seriously at all. My father was a civil servant. There was nothing obsessive or passionate [in his attitude to cinema]. He was much more in love with and devoted to classical music. He passed that on to me. He came from Pakistan, Lahore. Music was very alive in our home. But we lived in a town that was remote even by Indian standards. It was with that kind of extremely unformed mind, not knowing that cinema could be a serious form of expression, that I went to Harvard. It was only at the age of twenty or twenty-one that I understood cinema could be taken seriously. I never had any involvement with it [before then].

The scholarship at Harvard was for a general liberal arts degree. I really went there as an actor, to continue my work in experimental political theatre – but of course, at Harvard, there was none. It was all hoop skirts, musicals and *Oklahoma*. I was disillusioned and dropped the theatre. When I was twenty, I enrolled in a course in film-making. It was pretty hard to get into. Ten people only were admitted. I got in based on a series of still photographs I had taken a few months before. In this course, my professor showed the class *La Jetée*. If you think of the word 'epiphany', that was certainly the epiphany. There was another film that was interesting too, Jean Rouch's *Chronicle of Summer*, but *La Jetée* was the epiphany. I saw it in a classroom with maybe fifteen people and my professor. It was unforgettable. It crystallised that this [film-making] would be possible for me too. This I understood. This I was turned on by – the rigour, the economy, the photographic quality and the fact that you could make something big and impactful out of an idea, but not needing millions. *La Jetée* was unapologetically apocalyptical ... and vast. He [Marker] is one of those beacons – like Cartier-Bresson, like Pennebaker and Satyajit Ray. There are few people that just do what they do. They do it with sheer clarity.

I revisited *La Jetée* only a year ago before making *The Namesake*. A very important sequence in *The Namesake* is inspired only by *La Jetée*. I revisit it quite often. Marker has a line which he uses in *Sans soleil* about chronicling things that quicken the heart. Certainly, *La Jetée* always quickens my heart. For me, it was the first example – and the great example – of making something out of nothing. It creates a bridge to walk from photography to cinema.

La Jetée is a pretty sculptured piece of work. Over the years, what I have always remembered is the boldness of the photographic image – the way he uses the photographic image to create cinema, to create motion. It is really beautiful and not apologetic. When I think of it, I think of the quay, the jetty, the waiting for the plane to take off. The way he frames the plumpness of a child's calf between two railings. You don't even see the face of the child, just the calf. I also remember the romance with which he photographs, say, the nape of the neck of a woman. Half of the soundtrack is a heartbeat. I've seen an image of one of his crew members being made to run and Marker is photographing his heartbeat. I just love it. He demystifies everything and yet he creates opera – rigorous opera.

Being as interested then as I am now in still photography, it was the first evidence of how a bridge can be made from photography to cinema in a way that doesn't reduce anything but amplifies everything. It was an example of a piece of work that is photographic but deeply poetic and tremendously musical and political. All this in 29 minutes in a series of photographs that he created. Also, it taught me something I still use and that has become a cornerstone of my work and thinking, which is the use of sound and music. There is a tremendous boldness in his use of music – Wagnerian, operatic-type music. He just simply says Paris is blown up. Then he shows you a series of apocalyptic-type photographs about Paris in ruins. The operatic music was so bold and, at the same time, correct. It taught me right then and there to think big, even with tiny instruments. You don't have to have trumpets and men in suits to make large statements with the same impact. It's the power of the idea and how you use the medium. When I was preparing the DVD of my film *The Namesake* and I was putting together a series of images of photographers who inspired certain images in the movie, the final scene of *The Namesake* was inspired by *La Jetée*. I wrote to Mr Marker and asked if I could use his images. He wrote me this most eloquent letter. He is eighty-five years old saying what my film had meant to him. Even now, when I was watching *La Jetée* this week, it gave me such … the

La Jetée

La Jetée

way he filmed two people, a man and a woman in a frame, it is so revolutionary. It is brilliant but very musical – the way he shoots with his camera. You think you know how to shoot two people in a frame. Then you see Chris Marker doing it and it just teaches you anew.

We saw *La Jetée* at the beginning of that course. I was working photographically but I wanted to work with ideas, not just images. That film combined music, poetry and politics.

I am not an aficionado of science fiction at all. While I understand *La Jetée* is in that realm, now, when I revisit it, what also is stunning to me is how it includes things I am very directly involved with. For instance, Marker speaks in *La Jetée* of time as the ring of an ancient tree. There is that whole episode of the sequoia and the man and the woman pointing to different things that happen in time. That is something that I am interested in. Over the last fifteen years, I have become a gardener myself. The rhythm of nature has become a great teacher for me in my cinema as well. To revisit Marker and to see that direct allusion to cinema being involved with exploring the nature of time. That's something I didn't remember [from seeing the film] but now it seems to have a stunning kind of com-

plicity with my way of thinking. Also, what *La Jetée* gave me was how one could explore one's own identity through an idea. The character says this is where I come from, these images, this memory, that face, those gardens, that peacetime garden, these children – this is where I come from. That is very close to my work. That whole notion of being very personal in selecting the images of who you are and make the world that you inhabit. That is something I have been very freewheeling about, whether it is in the juxtaposition of East and West or whatever layering of that.

It must have been in 1977 that I saw *La Jetée*. The film was made in 1962. After that, I was in hot pursuit of anything else Marker would do. I've done the pilgrimage fairly actively. Marker is very reclusive. A close friend of mine just photographed his office, his studio in Paris. It's definitely an image like his films, dense and stacked, cats everywhere, old computers with completely new technology next to it.

Whether you are making a film on a big budget or a small budget, the best idea should always win. Marker teaches us good ideas – the ideas that are most effective. That's how I lean on him – for giving me that clarity. He is a talisman for me to keep within me. ”

Stephen Woolley

Zulu

(Cy Endfield, 1964)

Stephen Woolley
on the set of
The Crying Game
(1992)

Co-founder of Palace Pictures with Nik Powell, Woolley was a totemic figure in the British film industry of the 1980s – someone who made the journey from running a cinema and then a video distribution operation to becoming the most dynamic producer of the decade. He had big successes and also notable failures (the bold but ill-starred *Absolute Beginners*; d. Julien Temple, 1986). Palace eventually collapsed but Woolley regrouped and has remained a prolific producer, racking up credits from *Little Voice* (d. Mark Herman, 1998) to *TwentyFourSeven* (d. Shane Meadows, 1997). He is best known for his work with Irish director Neil Jordan, which stretches from Angela Carter adaptation *A Company of Wolves* (1984) to unlikely US sleeper hit *The Crying Game* (1992); from big-budget Tom Cruise movie *Interview with the Vampire* (1994) to Graham Greene adaptation *The End of the Affair* (1999). In 2005, he made his directorial debut with *Stoned*, about the fast life and suspicious death of Rolling Stones co-founder Brian Jones.

Born in 1956 into a working-class background in Islington, Woolley is a true cinephile – someone whose passion for watching movies led him to make them.

Stephen Woolley:

"When you watch movies as a child, the relationship between what is going on around you, what is happening to you when you are actually seeing a film, bears down on you as much as the movie itself. As you get older, especially in the modern day (where we watch films on DVD and download), the environment in which you are watching the movie doesn't come into play so much.

When I was fourteen or so, there was a course at school during which we would travel round to various cinemas in London, watch films and then discuss them the following week. This was at a grammar school called Owens in the Angel, Islington.

I had always been a real movie fan and would watch lots of films on my own in cinemas. I had a personality that tended to hide in books. Books were my obsession as a kid. I would always be found with my eyes in a book. My dad had a real ambition for me to read at an early age. He had learned to read in prison. He wasn't so much a working-class guy as a criminal-class guy. The part of London I came from, in Islington, was quite a tough world, although we never really saw that. He was a gambler. He spent most of his time gambling.

But as I was the eldest, the first-born and the son, he had a great ambition that I would learn to read and that this would be a big thing for me. I used to read quite an astonishing amount of mat-erial – Charles Dickens, Jennings, *Just William*, all sorts – from a very early age. We slept in one room and had a tiny little kitchen. The only escape, really, was books and the tiny TV we had. Although we didn't have lots of things like fridges and telephones and things, we did have a television. Anyone who had anything had a television. Most of the kids sat on the floor. But outside on the streets in Islington, it was lots of wonderful, leafy squares. I didn't have a cockney accent. I lost the accent really quickly because I went to a school with a lot of kids who were the children of professionals. Going to Thornhill School and finally Owens at the Angel, I was a bit of a fish out of water. My family were all originally from the East End and from the north of London and were working class. My uncles and aunts and nan were very much part of the real, old-fashioned fabric of Islington but I was this new hybrid. I was middle class in terms of the way I spoke and responded to things but I was from a very working-class background. I didn't really feel very comfortable at school, with these proper middle-class kids who had all these luxury things that I would never be able to afford and that my family would never be able to afford. But I never felt at home with the working-class kids because I didn't really want to sniff glue and go and do the things they wanted to do. And so I lost myself both in books and cinema. Cinema seemed to be a natural extension [of my reading].

The Rex Cinema was my local, which showed double bills. It was the cheapest cinema in the area. It later became the Screen on the Green where I worked. The Rex was a terrific home because they changed the programme every two days and they played mainly old 50s and early 60s movies that nobody else could be bothered to play but that the companies still had 35mm prints of. They would show a lot of the Dino De Laurentiis sword-and-sandal movies. They would also play a lot of British films, like the *St. Trinian's* films and the early *Carry On* films. Then, they would have the old Hollywood swashbuckler films. I remember seeing *The Crimson Pirate* at the Rex and sword-fighting home. It was fantastic. The Rex was a swashbuckling theatre. You had no idea what state the prints were going to be in. They would jump all over the place. A bit

later in the 60s, they showed *Von Ryan's Express* on a loop. They'd show those kind of movies. Then, on a Saturday night, I'd go with my cousins and uncles to see the big movie of the week – a James Bond film or whatever it was.

I remember *Zulu* in particular. All the kids were obsessed with *Zulu*. Everybody at my primary school had seen it and we re-enacted the scenes continually. That was a big influence for a kid. I think it was the incredible battle scenes [that so impressed us], the quantity of dying bodies and heroism. I think it was the heroism and this notion of the silent, endless attacks. It was a terrific adventure film. Like most kids, I saw movies like *Zulu* and *The Crimson Pirate* as great adventures.

At that time, a lot of cinema was to be found on TV, especially silent Laurel and Hardy and Charlie Chaplin. Movies like *Casablanca* were often at 7pm, at prime time. There were the old Hollywood greats. The Bette Davis and Jimmy Stewart movies were considered prime time. There would be late nights on Fridays where they would show Fred Astaire movies or Marx brothers movies. You'd have whole seasons of those movies. As a kid, you were imbued with cinema. Sunday afternoons would be *Dam Busters* and the old British

Zulu

movies, with the occasional Michael Powell. It was mainly the old propaganda films from the Second World War which still resonated in London. I think in the afternoons, I once saw *Great Expectations*. As I had been a Dickens fan, I actually read the book. What was interesting – and what had a very formative effect on my appreciation of cinema – was that although the David Lean film was an adaptation of a book, it was in itself a different thing. At a very early age, I realised that cinema didn't do to you just what a book could do. There was another level. It wasn't necessarily a better level but it was another place. What had happened with *Great Expectations* was that it had made a version of the book into a film that you could enjoy as much as, if not more than, when you were reading the book. I had always thought books were books and films were films and never the twain shall meet. But that acquainting of literature with cinema became obsessive for me, especially when I was doing my O levels. I was doing things at school like *Macbeth* and then I was seeing *Throne of Blood* [Kurosawa's film based on *Macbeth*].

At the start of the film course at school, one of the films I saw was Ingmar Bergman's *Wild Strawberries*. I hadn't really seen a Bergman up to that point (I was about fourteen). What was really interesting was that it was at the National Film Theatre. The strange 50s design of the screen as it pulled out pushed me into remembering the Buster Keaton movies that Michael Bentine would show [on TV] on a Friday night. They'd show short versions of the Keaton films: 20-minute versions of *The General*. I just loved Buster Keaton. For me, he was far above Harold Lloyd and Charlie Chaplin – the silent comics.

At school, when term was over, they would show old 8mm and 16mm Chaplin, Harold Lloyd and Laurel and Hardy movies and I'd always hope there was Buster Keaton. I loved the Michael Bentine shows and when the doors opened, I realised – oh, my God – they were actually filmed at this venue: the National Film Theatre. I immediately loved that cinema because I thought this is the cinema of Buster Keaton. Those doors meant to me Buster Keaton and Michael Bentine. When *Wild Strawberries* began, I was completely engrossed in it because I felt that somehow I had to be attentive to anything that came from that screen, anything from this strange place. *Wild Strawberries* is probably the first foreign-language film that showed me beyond the adaptation of books, there was another cinema – what was referred to as art cinema. It existed in its own universe without any reference to any literary background.

What was interesting about *Wild Strawberries* was that although it dealt with an old man facing death, thinking back on his life, there was a surreal quality and other-worldliness to the film which was to do with Scandinavia and Bergman's dabbling with surrealism and dabbling with time. This was another culture – the world that Bergman depicts was not a world I recognised at all from either films or books. There was something fresh and unusual compared to the other films I had seen – and it was not just that I had to read the subtitles. Seeing Bergman for the first time there, in that Buster Keaton world, was very important to me.

We saw a lot of films on that course, including *Battleship Potemkin*, which I think we saw at Queen Elizabeth Hall, and *Point Blank*.

Many years later, when I ran the Scala Cinema, I used to hire the Scala out to kids doing the same course. Kids would come along to see these films for the first time. The course hadn't changed that much either.

After that, I discovered the Rex (which became the Screen on the Green). I saw my first Chabrol films, my first Eric Rohmer films, my first Polanski films. That was where I saw Fellini. They had a late-night film show on BBC2 and I remember seeing *Seven Samurai*. That was amazing. It combined all of the things I loved. There was still the *Zulu/Captain Blood* adventure heroism and spectacular fight sequences.

I was reading about the auteur theory through *Time Out*. The first edition of *Time Out* was printed when I was fourteen or fifteen and it became my bible because it would not only analyse and critique films in the cinema but also on television. I would start to give points to the films I saw. I kept a log. The early reviewers of *Time Out* were very influenced by *Cahiers du cinéma* and Raymond Durgnat. I would go and buy Durgnat's *A Mirror for England* and the translated versions of *Cahiers* and realise that I needed to understand about this other cinema. What I learned was then applicable to other genres. I began to watch Hammer films that Terence Fisher had directed and I began to realise that they were much more interesting than the [Hammer] films made by other directors. One began to apply the same theories of auteurship to Michael Powell movies like *Colonel Blimp*. I could see they were different to other British films made during the war.

Hitchcock was someone who seemed to have crossed over into all areas that were interesting. Discovering Hitchcock for me was very strange. I used to have a deal with my parents that I would go to bed at a certain time in the early evening so that my sister would then go to bed. They would then wake me up to see the late-night film. That film was probably at 10 o'clock. It wouldn't be much later because in those days they would switch the TV off at 11.00 or 11.30. They were happy for me to sit on my own and watch these movies and then come back to bed. I saw the Universal horror films – *Frankenstein*, *The Wolfman* and the spin-offs. They were kind of kids' movies, really. There was nothing really too scary about them and they were very easy to cope with. During this series of films, they suddenly showed *Psycho*, which isn't a kids' film. It's very much an adult film. It shocked me to the core. Not only were the other films easy to dismiss because of the ridiculous situations and hokey make-up. They were horror films that were fantastical – they were fairy stories. *Psycho* was not a fairy story. It dealt in reality. As a kid watching it, there was a

reality in the film that I just bought into. I was really young, maybe ten or eleven. I didn't sleep for weeks afterwards. I couldn't say to anybody how much the films frightened me or talk to anybody about it because then I would be breaking the deal and they wouldn't wake me up again. That always conflicted me somewhat. It was also the power of cinema. Hitchcock in that period really did shake you up. My children have seen most of Hitchcock's and they watch them on a regular basis. They understand *Psycho* because they have seen *Rear Window* and they've seen *North by Northwest* and *Vertigo*. My kids are twelve, fifteen and seventeen. When they saw *Psycho*, they understood a Hitchcock film was a Hitchcock film. For me, it was another horror film – and it was a real moment of epiphany.

The odd thing was that I never once consciously thought, oh, I want to get into this business. I was very much interested in film as something that was incredibly entertaining, as an offshoot from books and reading. I really enjoyed being with other people but not being with other people. I never took girls on dates to the cinema as such, basically because the first time I tried to do it, it was a disaster. It was a double bill of *Drive, He Said* and *Fat City*. I was quite

Psycho (Alfred Hitchcock, 1960)

old by then, probably sixteen. I don't think you were supposed to go on a date to a double bill for hours, just sit there and watch the films. I realised very quickly that going with friends or potential girlfriends just wasn't going to work for me because I actually wanted to see the films more than anything else. I knew that all these people existed and I knew what they did – DPs, writers and directors. But it was only after beginning the Palace Video Label and pulling together the 'making of' documentary of *Merry Christmas, Mr Lawrence* that people like Jeremy Thomas and John Boorman suggested that I should consider producing. I hadn't ambitiously wanted to direct or produce. I really did come from a love and appreciation. That was what I was most about. When I flew to Tokyo for the first time to see *Merry Christmas Mr Lawrence*, it wasn't because I was trying to gazump the other distributors. It was because I genuinely wanted to meet Nagisa Oshima and to see this incredible collaboration – him making an English-language film with somebody like David Bowie. The idea of the movie sounded incredibly intriguing. And so, when Jeremy Thomas turned and told me, 'you're the only distributor that bothered to come to Tokyo', it was more because I had been driven by

Oshima than anything else. My love of cinema was quite pure.

Then I started the cinema [the Scala] but [my partner] Nik Powell persuaded me that we should start a video label. Then, it started to become more serious as we bought all rights for films like *Diva* and *The Evil Dead*. I realised that the video label wasn't going to work. I had taken a stake in the label and had bought all these movies and wanted to know why video didn't work. I worked out it didn't work because you had to have theatrical [distribution]. Moving into theatrical led to expanding the company, bringing more people on. It became more of an industry and very quickly, as I was acquiring films, I noticed that we had established a brand of new, younger, more exciting filmmakers. We were gazumped all the time because we had had such success. The idea of producing films was a commercial proposition. If I was able to judge on the basis of a script or a first screening if a film would have commercial potential, then surely I should be able to make a film from that script stage and keep all rights. That was what we attempted to do with *Company of Wolves*, which was to tackle elements of things we had done quite well with and make a film. *Company of Wolves* was inspired by the notion of Michael Powell and *Black Narcissus*. We wanted to keep it very foetid and all within a very claustrophobic forest plus taking Angela Carter's work and the Cocteau influence and make it a fantasy film rather than a straight-ahead horror film. The fairy tale was also very important. There were elements to the film that I had unconsciously absorbed through my apprenticeship of watching lots of movies. On that film, I directed second unit. It was definitely Neil Jordan's movie. I was just looking after the unit that was dragging up behind Neil, making sure they were doing well and reporting back to Neil – which I later discovered was kind of like directing second unit. I didn't know what a producer did and so I did everything. It turned out really well and it was a good experience. That was with Palace.

By producing *Company of Wolves*, I was blooded into the industry, as it were, at a fairly high level at a very young age. I was, I think, about twenty-seven. I had assimilated and absorbed much more than I had realised. By obsessing with this auteur thing and looking back at film-makers as disparate as Buñuel, Bresson and Roger Corman, I had short-circuited and short-cut quite a lot of what was happening with the business. Very quickly, I was making films like *Mona Lisa* and even *Absolute Beginners* – films that I thought would stand a chance commercially but were also making a statement in terms of subverting genre and giving Neil Jordan or Julian Temple an opportunity to make something that was part and parcel of their universe. It would be very hard to put my finger on a movie and say it was *Wild Strawberries* at the NFT or it was *Psycho* or it was *Zulu* or *Great Expectations* but if my memory isn't tricking me, those are the four moments. 〟

Martin Scorsese

The Red Shoes

(Michael Powell and
Emeric Pressburger, 1948)

Martin Scorsese
on the set of
Mean Streets
(1973)

In his autobiography *Million-Dollar Movie*, English director Michael Powell gives a tremendously vivid description of Martin Scorsese at work, halfway through the editing of his 1980 classic *Raging Bull*. Scorsese and his editor Thelma Schoonmaker are cutting the film in a cramped New York apartment. There are strips of celluloid everywhere. 'Film flowed out of the bedroom, across the sitting room and into the bathroom, and back again. There was no difference between day and night.'

Scorsese, as Powell surmised, is the most mercurial and intense film-maker of his generation. The Italian-American auteur (born in New York in 1942) originally planned to enter the Roman Catholic priesthood before being sidetracked by movies. His private life has been turbulent. His broken marriages and problems with cocaine in the 1970s are well chronicled, but he has seldom allowed anything to get in the way of his work. 'I don't expect much from people any more, and I don't really want them to expect much from me. Except when it comes to the work, where you're gonna get the best from me … that's the way it goes,' he once remarked.

Scorsese's films only fitfully succeed at the box office, but his virtuosity is such that the Hollywood system supports him regardless. As critic Ian Christie puts it it: 'His acknowledged artistry helps the studios feel like occasional patrons of the art they daily prostitute.' He is the most versatile of directors: capable of skipping from genre to genre and reinventing himself with each new movie. He has made musicals (*New York, New York*, 1977), melodramas (*Alice Doesn't Live Here Anymore*, 1974), gangster pics (*Mean Streets*, 1973, *Goodfellas*, 1990, *Casino*, 1995, *The Departed*, 2006), sumptuous literary adaptations (*The Age of Innocence*, 1993), religious films (*The Last Temptation of Christ*, 1988, *Kundun*, 1997) and even biopics (his Howard Hughes film *The Aviator*, 2004).

He is at once a superb visual stylist, capable of choreographing set-pieces worthy of his great idols Powell and Pressburger, and a consummate actor's director. Robert De Niro's brutal, mesmerising studies of characters like the psychopathic Travis Bickle in *Taxi Driver* (1976) or the self-destructive middleweight boxing champ Jake La Motta in *Raging Bull* are testament to the licence Scorsese allows his performers. In his movies, even the least likely actors often do exceptional work: think of Sharon Stone, superb as the femme fatale in *Casino*, or of Jerry Lewis in a rare straight role in *King of Comedy*.

Scorsese's *Gangs of New York* (2002), adapted from Herbert Asbury's 1927 *Informal History of the Underworld*, was a period gangster film with a reported budget of over $90 million. *The Aviator* and *The Departed* were also huge projects. However, as well as working on big-budget studio films, he has also made intimate documentaries (for example, his films on Bob Dylan and George Harrison and his forthcoming tribute to British cinema). Through the World Cinema Foundation, he is also highly active in the world of film preservation.

As Michael Powell noted, meeting him 'was like meeting a twister in Kansas. He talked a mile a minute, his mouth full of exclamations, explanations, opinions, questions and contradictions … here was a real king of the movies; he knew what he was doing and why he was doing it.'

Martin Scorsese:

"I saw *The Red Shoes* aged nine or ten. My father took me. Seeing it that first time was an overwhelming experience for me. My father, who worked in the garment district in New York, certainly wasn't an educated man but he did like films. For some reason, he took me to see *The Red Shoes*. I certainly don't think he was a ballet enthusiast. I believe that the film had picked up an audience here in America. Everyone was talking about it and so he wanted to see it.

My father liked the film very much too. We always used to talk about it. He liked it for its sense of mystery in terms of the character of Lermontov [the driven ballet impresario played by Anton Walbrook] and the kind of mystical endeavour of art that it showed. I don't say he said that. Certainly, he didn't. But there was something inevitable about what these people were doing. On his level, he would talk about the wonderful film it was and that it was a good show. It was obviously very different from many of the musicals that were coming out of America at the time in that the nature of the story had a very dark element to it. This was something unique, especially served up in such a beautifully made and crafted way.

I don't think my father understood the impact the film had on me at the time until years later, when he met Michael Powell. We all became sort of a family, my mother and father and Powell.

Over the years, I have been told that I am like Lermontov. I maybe tend to agree. I really don't know. There is something about the Lermontov character and the world that he controls that is, I guess, the pool that I go back to for sustenance. It has to do with the mystery of art – the mystery of the passion to create and the darker side which can take over. I think that will always be fascinating to me. It could very well have been an inspiration for the types of characters I tend to gravitate toward in the types of pictures I make.

And the first word that comes to mind about Moria Shearer in *The Red Shoes* is 'radiant', particularly in the way she was lit in the film and the angles that were used in her close-ups. The combination of actor/dancer seemed so natural for her. The nature of her physical build said so much about the character, even just a glance from her or a close-up.

There is something about the use of colour and the impact of the movement in the frame. It is to do with the high drama, even melodrama, within the lives of the characters and how seriously they took what they were doing – how seriously they looked at their art and experienced the art. It was also their actual journey in creating something and the difficulty they faced. You could really feel the work that was being done by these dancers and by Lermontov and by the Marius Goring character [the young composer]. It made it very visceral.

The colour, the way the film was photographed by the great Jack Cardiff, stayed in my mind for years. The film would be shown every Christmas on American television in black and white, but it didn't matter – we watched it. Even though it was in black and white on TV, we saw it in colour. We knew the colour. We still felt the passion – I used to call it brushstrokes – in the way Michael Powell used the camera in that film. Also, the ballet sequence itself was like an encyclopaedia of the history of cinema up to that point. They used every possible means of expression, going back to the earliest of silent cinema.

In the documentary I am making about British cinema, I have to approach it from my point of view, from what I experienced and how I experienced it. It was literally intertwined with American cinema. Watching British film was as natural as watching a Western. We began to understand the different genres of British cinema, whether it was *The Blue Lamp*, John Ford's *Gideon of Scotland Yard* [aka *Gideon's Day*], *An Inspector Calls* or Seth Holt's films, let alone the films by Joseph Losey or Basil Dearden or Ronald Neame. One of the problems with the documentary is knowing where to stop. These films were a major influence. There was the influence [on my work] of voiceover and narration and satire. In its very restrained way, *Kind Hearts and Coronets*, which was a big favourite among my family and the people watching television in the early 50s, was a film that influenced a great deal what I do with voiceover.

I met Michael Powell through [publicist] Michael Kaplan, who had worked with Stanley Kubrick and was beginning to work with Robert Altman. I and others had been asking about Michael Powell and Emeric Pressburger pretty much throughout the late 60s. We really couldn't find anything definitive written about them in any of the histories of British cinema. There was mention of *The Red Shoes* and that was basically it.

Among my colleagues – Coppola, of course, Spielberg and Brian De Palma

The Red Shoes

*Kind Hearts and
Coronets* (Robert
Hamer, 1949)

SCREEN EPIPHANIES

and pretty much everybody who was beginning to make films in the early 70s – whenever we spoke about a film and we couldn't remember the title, it was invariably something we had seen on television in black and white, written, produced and directed by Powell and Pressburger. We were all wondering who they were, where they were and whether they were still alive. If they were alive, we wanted to know what they were doing now. If we could meet them, we could ask them how they did that work together. That 'written, produced and directed by Michael Powell and Emeric Pressburger' is one of the most unique title credits in movie history, both sharing the same credit card.

Kaplan said, 'Oh, I know Michael – he is living in a trailer. If you'd like to meet him, I can arrange that.' I was in London for a couple of days and we met at this restaurant. He [Powell] sat across from me and we shared a glass of wine each. I was rather effusive about him and his work. I couldn't believe we had found him! We brought him up to date about the appreciation of his and Emeric's work among the younger film-makers. My friends and colleagues were still trying to find good colour copies of the work or at least extant copies of *A Canterbury Tale*. I do talk rather quickly.

I was excited. He seemed rather modest and somewhat taken aback. Quite honestly, I guess I spoke so much, I don't remember what he told me. We were so excited to find him and to know he was still alive, at least trying to work.

Powell had gone from making 'quota quickies' [low-budget British films] in the 30s on to his collaboration with Pressburger and then on to a film like *Peeping Tom*. When I was at Washington Square College, which was part of New York University at the time, there was a very, very small film department. *Peeping Tom* was shown for a week or two in black and white. It became a legendary film. Even if people had missed it, they talked about it. It really fed directly into a wonderful film made by Jim McBride at the time, who was also a student, called *David Holzman's Diary*. *Peeping Tom* was one of the key influences on that. He [Powell] was really influencing an entire generation.

He [Powell] was living in this small trailer. It looked like an Airstream. He was trying to work. Now, looking back, I know he was in dire circumstances with finances and pretty much everything else.

I was more of a close friend of Michael Powell than of Pressburger. Michael came to New York. He came to

California when I was living there. We were around each other a great deal of the time. I only met Emeric a few times. It's hard for me to comment on their collaboration. I don't think anybody could have a fair sense of how something like that evolved. The results are so extraordinary. We look at that remarkable title card that says 'written, produced and directed by' and we realise that one couldn't do without the other. Pressburger brought a certain European sensibility to the work. That fascinates me because it's not only British. Michael grew up in the South of France. Emeric Pressburger's home country was Hungary. From what I read and know, they worked very closely and well together and the results were quite extraordinary – masterpiece after masterpiece.

I keep coming back to *The Red Shoes*. It's shown on Turner Classic Movies. I find that if I come back from shooting a film at 3am from a night shoot or at dawn and it's on, I find it is difficult to got to sleep. It is a film that I continually and obsessively am drawn to. It was very hard to see good colour copies of the film. I sought out whatever theatre they were playing in. Eventually, we obtained colour television sets and we saw it at least on colour on TV. The big prize was to get a good 16mm colour print. That was like a major coup to get that – or, at least to see it if not to own one. That become a kind of obsessive search.

The funny thing about it is the nature of possessing a print of the film. It's not about the celluloid. It's not about the print. It's about the nature of the film itself and how the film changes in my mind when I see it or it changes in my heart when I see it. I always say that film doesn't really exist. When you see it, it's just reels of celluloid. One has to project the film. You need electricity. Then the film plays out in your mind and your heart. It continually does that for me.

Over the years, looking at *The Red Shoes* and seeing the world it depicted, I have begun to see the analogy with the world I am in. It keeps giving me the energy to keep moving on. As far as Michael and Emeric are concerned, volume two of Michael's autobiography is quite unique. He talks not just about his period of success but also about when things went bad. It is interesting to see how the world changed at that time and to follow the political moves he made. After *The Tales of Hoffmann*, things became more difficult. Then, *Peeping Tom* was the finish. In any event, from reading the autobiography and knowing Michael from 1975 until 1990 [when he died], I think he and Pressburger were as skilled as politicians as they could have been in that world. Working for J. Arthur Rank, they were able to create this string of masterpieces. That changed. It's the nature of the way the world has changed now. Can you survive with a different set of political circumstances? That was very difficult for them. **" "**

Index

Main entries (for a director or an epiphanic film) are in **bold** type. Entries in *italics* denote illustrations. Titles of foreign-language films are given in the form used by the individual contributor, cross-referenced where appropriate.

List of Illustrations

While considerable effort has been made to correctly identify the copyright holders, this has not been possible in all cases. We apologise for any apparent negligence and any omissions or corrections brought to our attention will be remedied in future editions.